JOHN & EVE

06.

Pete

OUTSIDE LOOKING IN

PETE MITCHELL

Alias STRATMASTER

THE DERWENT PRESS
Derbyshire, England

www.derwentpress.com

OUTSIDE LOOKING IN
By
Pete Mitchell

alias
Stratmaster

www.stratmaster.co.uk

© 2006 Peter Mitchell

All Rights Reserved.

No part of this book may be reproduced in any form or by any means, electronic or mechanical, including photocopying, recording or by any information storage and retrieval systems, without the written permission of the copyright owner.

ISBN 1-84667-011-X

Cover art and book design by:
Pam Marin-Kingsley
www.far-angel.com

Published in 2006
by
The Derwent Press
Derbyshire, England
www.derwentpress.com

'OUTSIDE LOOKING IN' is dedicated to all the very talented musicians, that I have had the pleasure to work with, while being on the 'OUTSIDE LOOKING IN' and to all my loyal listeners over the years.

I hope my CD titled 'Cutting The Mustard' will express my personal feelings, and also show my absolute passion for the BLUES!

Keep On Rocking,

Pete Mitchell

alias
Stratmaster

CONTENTS

	PAGE
FOREWORD	1
CHAPTER 1. HOOKED	3
CHAPTER 2: BOOZE, BLUES AND FLOWERS	19
CHAPTER 3: MEDITERRANEAN MADNESS	34
CHAPTER 4: BITING THE BULLET	47
CHAPTER 5: SOMETHING BREWING	54
CHAPTER 6: THE ACID TEST	64
CHAPTER 7: FINAL DRIVE	73
SUPPLEMENTARY BENEFITS	88
LANDLORD'S LEXICON	90

Pete Mitchell *alias* Stratmaster

Foreword

Life has its price, and one way or another; we will all have to pay for it. On invitation, I went to see a famous clairvoyant named Madame Faye. Her prediction of the assassination of President J.F. Kennedy brought her worldwide recognition. I was a total skeptic, and we had never met before. In retrospect, everything she told me about my past was true, and what was stunning beyond belief was the fact that all the major events in this book were predicted in detail by Madame Faye to me at her house in the summer of 1966. The last thing she said to me was, 'you will be successful with your music, but only after a long, hazardous journey, and you'll have to sacrifice everything for it'.

For most musicians, it's usually a case of playing for fun. Some play professionally, and others make the 'Big Time'. I take the view that a real musician is rarer still. He doesn't play to survive—HE SURVIVES TO PLAY.

My only credentials for having this point of view are some thirty years playing on the pub and club scene, and still gigging strong.

OUTSIDE LOOKING IN

Pete Mitchell *alias* Stratmaster

CHAPTER 1
HOOKED

On a fine Saturday morning in the summer of 1957, something happened to me that would determine my thoughts, my feelings, and, more profoundly, my whole life. I was just eleven years of age, with bags of energy and enough imagination to share with the street. Having had quite a strict Christian upbringing, certain principles were formed within my character at a very early age. Some of them I am grateful for, and others I probably could have done without.

What happened on that magical morning was an experience incredibly powerful, and truly a force to be reckoned with. As I went outside into the backyard, I could hear a strange sound. I climbed up over the rubble and reached the end wall. This divided my known world from the real world beyond. Anxiously, I scuffed up the six-foot high wall, and my ears experienced the most beautiful sound I'd ever heard. On the other side of the wall stood an amazing character with sideburns and drapes, it was a real teddy boy. He was about sixteen years of age and he was strumming his acoustic guitar with much enthusiasm while looking at his reflection in the window. Instantly, I was HOOKED, and a message went from my brain to every nerve end in my body. A voice was saying to me, 'I want to do that' and, 'I want to make that noise'. I knew there and then that I must have a guitar and learn how to play it.

I was born in Liverpool in 1946, under the star sign of Leo. My mother was a Scouse and my father was a Londoner. When I was four years of age, they moved down to London. On arrival, they moved in with my grandmother, who had her own house in Battersea. My only sister, Pamela, was a year older than me and she was a nice kid who always used to side with me whenever I got into trouble. As a youngster, I was extremely mischievous and was always getting into some kind of mess. Usually I would mix with the older kids. The funny thing was, nine times out of ten, I would be the one branded as the ringleader. Sure enough, I would have to take the blame, whether I was guilty or not. The older boys would tell my father that I was the one causing all the trouble and encouraging them.

When you are in this position, it's not very long before you realise that you have got to be as crafty as them and keep one jump ahead. My father was quite a strict man, who has since mellowed out considerably. At that time, he was very worried about me. He wanted his son to behave in a way that I thought was impossible. Everything I did always seemed to be wrong, and yet, everything my sister did was nearly always right.

I went to a very basic junior school called, 'Latchmere Road', most of the kids there were from poor families with pretty rough backgrounds. In order to give the kids something to do after school, they had a scheme called 'play centre'. This meant that parents could either have some time to themselves or they could collect their kids after work at six o'clock and take them home with them. It also meant that the kids were not roaming around the streets for hours on end after school. Even at this early age, I was a bit of a rebel. I hated going to 'play centre'. I used to disappear and run off to end up roaming around the school. My father would come to the 'play centre' to pick me up, but I would be outside somewhere, probably climbing on the school roof. It is no wonder that they were so worried about me. Funny thing is, at that time I was called a very naughty boy, now, some forty years later, its just 'boys will be boys'. My parents were obviously very concerned about their son but, in retrospect, I know that it was the Victorian attitude that I found irritating and unacceptable.

At this point in time my parents were trying very hard to encourage their eleven-year-old son to take his schoolwork seriously. My father would say to me, 'you have got to work hard and study', and 'concentration is the secret'. My sister, being older than me, would listen to my father and would always get good results at school. Very quickly, I realised that if the guitar were to have a place in my life, then it would have to take the place of other things. Unfortunately, my parents didn't see eye to eye with me on this vital matter. Very quickly, this became a serious issue, and there I was, making my first guitar out of old orange boxes, using fishing tackle for the strings. I banged some nails into the end of the neckpiece to emulate the machine heads of the guitar. The fact that this apparatus was totally unplayable did not matter a jot. The important thing was that I had to be able to wear it around my neck and strum it, in imitation of my Teddy boy neighbour.

Whenever I got the chance, I would gulp down my breakfast, get dressed quickly, and strap on my roller skates. I would grab my imitation guitar and make a beeline for my best friend's house. He lived in the next street from me, and I would serenade everyone on the way round to his house, whether they liked it or not. Even at that early age, I realised

OUTSIDE LOOKING IN

the impact a guitar had on people and how they would all look up and take notice of me. Looking back now, I'm sure that most of them thought I was mad, and must have wondered what on earth I was doing posing with these bits of wood nailed together and hanging around my neck. The point is, it didn't bother me in the slightest. What did bother me was the fact that I couldn't get a recognisable sound out of this thing. My biggest audience so far was a bus shelter in Battersea, full of people waiting for the bus. I thought they needed entertaining, but they were obviously disappointed with the lack of musical content.

I was in my last year at junior school and I didn't play an instrument. My only saviour at this time was my love for singing. I never missed a music class, and it was the only lesson that I really loved and got excited about. I am sure that being brought up by musical parents had a lot to do with it. I belonged to the school choir and I would go to choir practice in and out of school hours. This was how I released my frustration. My heart was in my music and, one way or another, I knew I would eventually master the art of playing an instrument. At this age, the only instruments available to me were the piano, recorder and, later, the violin. Schools didn't teach guitar at this time, and I'm pretty sure they thought it was an instrument that would give kids the wrong influence. It was sort of taboo, due to the rock and roll element. I felt quite certain that nobody else around me realised just how important and popular this instrument was going to be. Fortunately for me, I did!

I didn't respond to any of the instruments available, but I was very involved with the school choir. My music teacher, known to us as Old Man Brookes, was brilliant. He could play the piano like Bruce Hornsby. I used to ask him 'Why do you play all these hymns and school songs when you can play Rock and Roll music?' He would say quite simply, 'It's my job, and someone has got to teach you kids how to sing carols'. This was his way of saying that somebody had to teach us the basics of music. I sang with the choir for a couple of years and was given the chance to sing the lead part in one of the Christmas services. I was very pleased with this, as the leading girl singing opposite me was a year older, and I was rather fond of her. Her name was Rose, and I think that she was the first girl I fell in love with. We were both sopranos but unfortunately, that was about the only thing we did have in common. Her mother said that she could sing with me, but that was all. She was told to concentrate on her schoolwork, and she was not allowed out after school. Later, I saw her out with a boy who was a lot older than I was, and I also discovered that she was pregnant. In fact, she was kicked out of the choir and that was that. Sadly, it was the last time that anyone saw her.

My first taste of schoolboy success was with the choir. I was singing my solo piece at the local church service, where apparently Old Man Brookes had invited the choirmaster from Westminster Cathedral. Unknown to me, I was being vetted for the possibility of singing in the Westminster Choir. I passed the audition, and after a good chat with my father, I decided not to join after all. My choirmaster was upset and tried hard to change my mind, but I knew that what I really wanted to sing was Rock and Roll and not Christmas carols. One of the most significant things in my life was taking place at this time, and it would have been a disaster for the choir. My voice was starting to break, and when it did, I knew it would be the end of my soprano days. It was farewell Jerusalem, and greetings to 'ROXVILLE'.

In the late fifties and early sixties, pop music was developing and becoming a lot more accessible to the teenagers. The radio had its pirate stations, and they were playing American music. This was pushing the music scene towards a Rock and Roll explosion and became an important part of our social activities. Youth clubs were springing up and for the first time, we were seeing live venues in our own town. Up until then, I only had my music books to gloat over, like the 'Shadows' and folk song books. Day after day, I would look at their photographs, dreaming of playing on stage with a band. Entrenched in my mind at this time was a particular photograph of the 'Shadows' on stage in Stockholm. Little did they know that I was there with them, certainly in spirit.

I managed to muddle through with my schoolwork until I was fourteen years old. My father was very concerned for me at this time, because he knew I was thinking for myself a lot more and had reached an age where my own views were becoming far more important to me. Until now, I'd always had an average school report, sometimes they were even worse. I was very nervous about taking reports home and letting my parents see what I had been up to for the past term. The amount of information revealed in a report was always staggering. I would usually get marks B & C for most subjects, I would always get top marks for music, PE and woodwork. Every time I showed my report to my parents, they would say to me, 'You have got to try harder with your main subjects'. My father would say to me, 'Mathematics, English, History and Geography are extremely important'. This carried on for a while but unfortunately; I would be miles away, thinking about other things.

My concentration in class was always on my music and seldom on what it should have been. At the end of the report form, there was always a space for remarks by the form teacher. Comments usually read, 'Peter must try harder', and,

Pete Mitchell *alias* Stratmaster

'We know that he has the ability, but for some reason he will not use it'. Having had a few reports like this and having gone through embarrassment and distress with my parents, I decided to please them. I would show them they hadn't given birth to a total pea brain. I would make one final effort in my last year at school to do something to make them feel proud of me. When a son is bordering on the edge of rebellion, it must be terribly painful for the parents. They are uncertain as to which way he will go. I loved my folks a lot, and I had a great deal of respect for them. I sat for my final examinations and not only did I surprise my parents with the results, I surprised myself. I got A & B marks for all the subjects, including Mathematics and English. I actually came 'top of the class' for the very first time. Usually, I came about twelfth place in a class of thirty.

My parents were delighted with the result, and I think they were pleased because I had listened to them and made a serious effort. They knew that I had it in me and that the teachers had been right all along. When I talk to my mother and father about it now, they both admit that it was due to the lack of concentration and that all my thoughts and efforts went into my music. After a while, I was thinking about one thing and one thing only, I desperately wanted a guitar.

Often, I would try to make myself a tunable guitar but, for whatever reason, I would always fail miserably. Others outside the family must have noticed my frustration and persistent obsession for the guitar. Soon, another significant event for me was about to happen. Some friends of my parents witnessed my frustration and said that they had an old acoustic guitar, and would I like it? My father, trying to be polite, wondered if it was such a good idea. He thought that it might be like waving a red rag at a bull. I very quickly reassured him that this was a brilliant idea, and could we put it into motion as soon as possible, please? After quite a lengthy talk with me, I seem to remember that part of the deal was for me to promise that I would not let this guitar take over and become more important than anything else.

I understood my father's point of view and I sympathized with him. On the day they brought the guitar round to my house, however, my life changed and all my promises faded into oblivion. There I was, fourteen years of age and terribly excited, reaching out and taking hold of what I remembered as the real thing. A real guitar with real parts on it, looking exactly the same as the guitars I had gloated over in magazines. It was the perfect shape and, above all, when you strummed the strings, it made the right noise. At last, after nearly three years of dreaming and being disappointed with cheap, unplayable, so-called guitars from junk shops, I finally had the reason for life in my hands.

Being the proud owner of an acoustic guitar very quickly pushed me into gear. It became obvious to me that owning it was the easy bit. I remember my mother would say to me, 'Pete, you must not get so upset. Just keep trying, because practice makes perfect'. I had great respect for my mother, for she played the piano quite well. She thought that I would learn to play better eventually, as long as I had the right attitude. These were hard times for me. I would lock myself away in my bedroom for days on end, trying to get some kind of acceptable sound from this thing. Even the poor old cat decided that he had suffered enough and left home for a while. Occasionally, I would get annoyed and hit my pillow with my guitar, knowing that I would never seriously damage it. In retrospect, I suppose it released some of the frustration and in fact made me even more determined. In time, I realised that tuning the guitar was something very important to the sound process. At that time, we didn't have electronic tuners on the market. You either had an ear for music and pitch, or you didn't. With more encouragement from my mother, I eventually believed that I had been blessed with an ear for music. In time, I mastered the art of tuning by ear. Later I realised that this was a real plus.

Having spent two years learning and copying, I had improved my playing techniques, but still wanted to play much better. More to the point, I wanted to be taken seriously by everybody, including my family and friends, as to my commitment to the guitar. At the beginning, I remember buying my first tutor book called 'Play In A Day', by Bert Weedon. This was far more exciting than any comic or 'Boys Own' annual. It was a new language with endless possibilities. Most of all, there was nothing quite like playing those first few chords. Later, when reasonably satisfied I could string a few chords together and strum a so-called tune, I had no time to lose. Suddenly my whole vocabulary became guitars, chords and Rock and Roll. Often I would go to my local record shop in Clapham Junction where the new 45s were on sale. Every now and then the shop would get a new songbook in. I must have bought dozens of those early books and records. The books usually had traditional folk songs in them, and there were a very limited number of alternative books available at that time. Though the 'Shadows' first wet my palate for playing on stage, I was never interested in just playing instrumentals.

Unknown to me at that time, there was a huge pop revolution waiting around the comer. In the early sixties, bands like the 'Beatles' and the 'Rolling Stones' were surfacing. We were also about to experience the 'Mersey Sound' while, at the same time, there were English bands playing American blues, which was tagged 'Rhythm and Blues'. This was a real breath of fresh air for the guitarist. It forced the development of electric guitar playing outside of the acoustic folk approach, and it became an alternative to the disciplined instrumental type of playing similar to the 'Shadows'. Something I discovered at the start of my career was the fact that it was very important to have flexibility and be able to put my own character into what was being played and, at the same time, to feel an inner satisfaction. I have always had the opinion that the feel is far more important than anything else, particularly with the electric blues guitar. By its very nature, it needs expression and the right touch. The 'Rhythm and Blues' music seemed to have the scope for this approach, whereas the 'Mersey Sound' had much more focus on melody and vocal harmony. This was a rich musical menu for me to feast on, and I knew that I would need plenty of time to digest it.

Noticing what was happening around me was becoming instinctive, I was always trying to find out what was going on musically. As far as the live aspect was concerned, I was well aware of the clubs and who played them. At the time of the 'Mersey Sound' explosion, I was going to folk clubs and playing with one or two folk guitarists. My first guitar had now become unplayable, and I became very interested in the folk club scene. Eventually, I made friends with a guitarist who played on the folk circuit, and he introduced me to some of the more established folk guitarists who were around at that time.

Obviously, I was very impressed with these players. They would play the clubs in England and then go and play in Europe, trying to scratch a living there. This was the first time I realised that making money from playing was definitely the exception to the rule. For the majority, it was necessary to enjoy playing above all else. I was fortunate enough to play with some of these guitarists. I eventually received my first professional guitar. This guitar was an old Gibson acoustic six-string, with an ebony fingerboard and an incredible sound. At the vulnerable age of eighteen, I realised that I had just moved up into the big boys' league. I knew only too well that the offer of joining a band would be the thin end of the 'Rock and Roll' wedge. Later I was to discover that I would be the rhythm guitarist and vocalist in such a project.

My best friend, Jimmy, had helped me to make my first imitation guitar. As a kid, he had encouraged me with most of my schoolboy dreams. On one occasion, he asked if I would like to go with him to a gig. It was a Friday evening, and the gig was being held in a school hall just around the corner from where we lived. There had been a lot of talk about this event and everyone for miles around knew about it. I said that I would go, mainly because they were having a live band, and not just playing records. Jimmy called for me at seven o'clock that evening, and I was ready to go. I was wearing what was considered trendy clothes at that time, Chelsea boots, flares, and a Beatle jacket. My style was very much the 'Mod' image, even though I had been mixing with Beatniks and Folkies, who were living down on the riverboats. Anyway, we got to the gig at Surrey Lane School and it was very crowded. I can remember distinctly two things at that gig, the first was the band's gear, and the second was the stage.

While standing in line waiting for the band to come on, I was getting very nervous. I was very anxious for them, but then they started to play. I felt an immediate relief and a positive rush of adrenaline flow through my veins. I remember I used to get that same feeling every time I looked at those early photographs of the 'Shadows' on stage. I felt as if I was part of the band, giving them my full support, even though we had never met before. My enthusiasm must have filled the hall, for I was terribly excited about it all. As luck would have it, the singer was struggling with his voice, and he was definitely not cutting it. I could see the band was getting more uncomfortable as the gig went on and the audience was slowly losing interest. In view of this problem, the band played instrumentals by the 'Shadows', and were very reluctant to play any more songs with their singer. Jimmy turned to me and said, 'Why don't you get up and sing with the band?' I said, 'I would like to, but they don't know me, and we have never played together before'. As quick as a flash, he told me that he had chatted with them in the interval, telling them that I knew some of their songs by the 'Beatles' and 'Rolling Stones', and that I would get up onto the stage in the second half and sing with them. Still in a state of shock with the adrenaline pumping round, I finally agreed to a quick chat with the band. It became very apparent from that moment on that I was either going to fulfill my wildest dream or I was going to be at the centre of a very embarrassing event. With fingers crossed and all the encouragement in the world from Jimmy, I got up onto the stage. The band very kindly introduced me, and I couldn't help but notice out of the comer of my eye that their singer had skulked off to the back end of the hall.

Singing a mixture of 'Beatles' songs, including 'Twist and Shout', 'I Saw Her Standing There' and 'Money', coupled with some 'Rolling Stones' songs such as, 'Come On' and 'I Wanna Be Your Man', I was in seventh heaven. This was definitely the closest I had been to playing in front of such a large crowd. I managed to control my nerves, and when I heard that first burst of applause, I just couldn't believe it. Until now, I had been used to the folk club audiences, who were usually laid back. Some of them were so laid back, in fact, that they were completely out of it. After the gig, Jimmy said that I had cut it and that the band was well pleased. He was great, and we still keep in touch from time to time.

Pete Mitchell *alias* Stratmaster

The band at the 'Surrey Lane' gig that I stood in for was called the 'Centaurs', and the leader turned out to be a decent guy. He asked me if I would join his band on a permanent basis, and I told him that I would need some time to think about it. Well, guess what? The very next day I got in touch with him and accepted his offer. We rehearsed regularly in an old school hall and, within months, we had an act with a good repertoire. We were also playing some original songs. I remember that one of the highlights with this band was headlining a gig at the 'Essoldo' in Clapham Junction, now called the 'Grand'. My first taste of recording was with these boys, and we recorded some songs in the Regent Sound Studios on Denmark Street, then known as 'Tin Pan Alley'. The 'Rolling Stones' were recording an album there too, at that time. I can remember a huge Neuman microphone being placed in front of me, it was such a contrast from the Reslo ribbon microphones that we used on stage. I found out, some fifteen years later, that the lead guitarist with the 'Centaurs' went on to teach guitar and to work for Southern Television. We actually met again by pure chance at a party in Surbiton, in 1979. If my memory serves me correctly, the 'Centaurs' also auditioned for 'Opportunity Knocks'. This was a television talent show. We were close, but unfortunately, not close enough. I must add that while working with the 'Centaurs', I was playing rhythm guitar and singing lead vocals. Being the front man was a huge responsibility for me, and a real challenge. I worked with the 'Centaurs' for a couple of years, mainly in the pubs and clubs, occasionally we would gig the colleges.

We played around the local area, mainly in the youth clubs. At that time, there were a lot of youth clubs around, and we were always keen to play in them if we could. The best thing about the youth clubs were the large crowds that went to them. Normally, they were held in church halls, and sometimes they would use public halls or town halls. They were usually good venues with a stage, and they always had a good dance floor, with curtains and stage lights. Most of those early venues were far nicer than the majority of the pubs around today. I can remember the 'Centaurs' on one occasion going to one of the roughest clubs around, called, the 'Darley Road' Club'. We were up on the stage giving it everything when suddenly, the whole place turned into a riot.

The 'Junction Mob' was there wrecking the place, fighting with the 'Darley Road' boys, who were on their home ground. It was just like a clip from one of those Wild West movies, where you see the whole place smashed to pieces, with arms and legs everywhere. We carried on playing. When the drummer was coming to the end of his solo, he called out 'Wipeout' (apt title) and suddenly, we heard a huge crash. It happened so quickly. I saw a chair fly past my eyes, faster than the speed of sound. Immediately, the drums went dead and when I looked around, I could see that the chair had gone right through the bass drum skin, practically demolishing the poor old drummer's kit. That was it for us. Fortunately, we were escorted out of the club by the bouncers, who eventually sorted out the riot and got things back under control. Everyone I looked at had cuts and bruises, even the girls had joined in.

There was another major shock at this time when the 'Centaurs' were playing at one of their pub gigs, in the Garratt Lane area of Wandsworth. This was a small pub, called 'The Wagon and Horses', and it had a very friendly landlord. Both he and his wife were Irish, and most of the punters were too. We had been booked to play for them on a night when they decided to have the television on without the sound. There we were again, singing 'Love Me Do' and so on, when suddenly the landlord ran up to the television in the middle of the song and turned the sound up full blast. We had no choice but to stop, and, to our amazement, we were witnessing a news flash

Pete Mitchell *alias* Stratmaster

showing the assassination of the American President, John F. Kennedy. Everybody in that pub was crying and shouting, and I have never seen such a disturbed crowd, they were all shell-shocked. We were young and I have never forgotten that night, it certainly was a night to remember.

The 'Centaurs' had a management team comprised of two brothers, who were both in their late twenties. One did the managing and the other brother, who bought the van, took care of the road managing. For a while, they made a good team, but when they realised that a quick return for their investment was not going to be quite so quick, things started to fall apart. This was to be another basic lesson for me to learn about the 'Rock and Roll' business. I just wanted to play, money or no money. It was the playing that mattered.

With so much enthusiasm in the early stages of the band, we opened our own club. It was on a Wednesday evening at the local church hall, and we called it the 'King Bee'. The vicar was delighted, and I don't think he had ever seen his church so packed on a Wednesday evening before. The fact that we paid him rent for the hall pleased him immensely. He took a real liking to 'Rhythm and Blues', and we couldn't do a thing wrong in his eyes. This was an invaluable experience for me, because it enabled me to see what was involved in being a self-contained act that had to set up its own gear and sound system. We even had our own stage clothes because we felt that our image was very important, especially for live audiences.

With human nature being what it is, I could feel the need for a change. I knew most of the local bands around at that time and I decided to play with some of them, but never really got a decent bite at the cherry in the 'Pop World'. Even though I knew that I probably wouldn't be the next Elvis Presley, I still realised that I could be a good player, even with-

OUTSIDE LOOKING IN

out success visible. I also knew that I was a musician who regarded his playing as important as his very next breath of fresh air. Unfortunately, I was often surrounded by other musicians who only talked about success, and very little else. Later on, I discovered that most of them proved to be far less creative than I was and, eventually, they disappeared from the scene.

CHAPTER 2
BOOZE, BLUES AND FLOWERS

While approaching my twentieth birthday, I had noticed that my feet were becoming increasingly restless, and I could feel the urge to travel. At this time, I was playing with a south London band, called the 'Boots'. I had a lot of fun with this outfit, and, being young and foolish, I got involved with the girl singer. She was working with an act called 'Les Denvers', who were signed to Polydor records. One thing led to another and I suddenly found myself engaged to her. This created a problem, and I had to find a way of solving it. My intention was to play music and earn money, and to travel and see the world. While trying to do this, I also convinced myself that I really should get married and spend the next few years preparing for all of this. This was certainly a tall order, and as luck would have it, I found what I thought might be the ideal solution.

My plan was to try to join the Merchant Navy. You have to remember that in the late sixties, traveling was very fashionable and cruise ships were having a field day. I was so impressed with the stories I had heard from friends about paradise islands and beautiful girls that this seemed to be just what I was looking for. I knew that if I enlisted, it would only

OUTSIDE LOOKING IN

be a matter of days before I would be playing again with a band in some form or another. I thought about joining the Merchant Navy for a few weeks, talking it over with my girlfriend for a while. As long as my reason for joining was solely for getting the money to pay for the wedding and somewhere to live, she said it would be all right. Unfortunately, I have to be honest. I was pushing the wedding and the settling down part of it right into the back of my mind.

Having made the decision to join the Merchant Navy, I needed to enroll. At that time, there were two ways of entry into the Navy, and one was as a seaman. For a beginner, this would mean some training at sea school. The second way 'in' was as a steward or a waiter in the catering department. I decided that the best way for me was via the catering route, and so off I went to the London docks, in search of a ship. On arrival at the docks, I saw various ships loading and unloading their cargo.

Seeing the interior lights shine through the portholes on this bitter cold night had an amazing effect on me. It was a magnetic feeling, and I wanted to jump on board right there and then. I felt drawn to the snug and cosy atmosphere that appeared to be so hypnotic. Soon I was to discover that this was not the way to get a job on a ship. The HM customs official informed me that I was trespassing, and if I didn't remove myself from the dock area immediately, I would end up being keel-hauled. (I thought that went out with Nelson). This was my first taste of naval discipline, and I came out of the docks a lot quicker than I went in.

My home at this time was in Tooting, where I was living with friends in a house we called, 'Beclands'. Sometimes there would be a dozen or more of us, living under the same roof. 'Beclands' belonged to my friend's parents, and was definitely one of the most people-friendly homes I had ever lived in. Olive, the mother, worked day and night coping with the chores, and we would all muck in with the various jobs that had to be done. We would spend many a winters' night playing guitars and singing, and sometimes, we would set up the drums and give the neighbours a real treat. One thing that Olive mastered was the ability to cook a superb Sunday roast. Her Yorkshire pudding was sheer delight. The funny thing was, the house was always packed on Sundays. I'm sure we had half of the street in there at weekends.

In the spring of 1966, I finally had a plan to try to enlist into the Merchant Navy. I discovered that the only way to get in would be to go directly to a shipping line and see if they had any vacancies. I decided to take the catering route, and selected a couple of shipping lines. I spent a few weeks getting some character references together, because I knew that it would be impossible to get in without them. Fortunately for me, I didn't have a police record. I went to the P&O shipping line first, to see if they would employ me. P&O sailed around the world, unlike other companies that just sailed to parts of the world. The thought of the Caribbean, Australia, Japan, the Middle East and Hawaii was enough to get me going. P&O sailed to all these places, and, as I was about to discover, they also sailed to some beautiful islands. You have to remember, that this was a big improvement on Brighton, Southend and Battersea.

Dressed to impress, I went to London and arrived at the P&O offices, and was very pleased with the friendly reception they gave me. I was shown into an office and interviewed by a guy with an amazing suntan. In my mind, all I could think about were Hawaiian Islands with hula-hula girls, and me lying on a sun-drenched beach. It's not easy trying to answer serious questions with all this going on in one's head. There I was, a devoted musician, having to pretend that a career in the

OUTSIDE LOOKING IN

Merchant Navy was the most important thing in my life, not daring to mention to anyone my passion for music. The interview was a success. I was told to report to the Merchant Navy offices in London, and they, in turn, would arrange for me to have a thorough medical. While waiting in line for the 'cough and drop' routine, unknown to me, I was chatting to some future members of my next band. I went back to my mother's home in Battersea for a few weeks, waiting for my official entry papers to come through. I wanted to spend some time with my family before sailing off into the unknown.

For a while, it was just a matter of killing time because I didn't know exactly when I would be leaving, hopefully, for the other side of the world. I came from an area in London where the council was still trying to sort out the bomb damage. The German raids in the Second World War caused these bomb sites. Just thinking about traveling the world and seeing these different countries, made me feel good. I would sit up late at night chatting to a friend of mine, who joined the Merchant Navy about a year before me. They put him on an old tub called the 'Northern Star', which belonged to the Shaw-Saville line, and he used to sail to South Africa. After hearing about his exploits, I would be even more fired up and keener still to get away.

I am sure that my friend Kenny had a big influence on me, and listening to his stories just fuelled my imagination at that time. Kenny was a gambler and he reassured me it was a life full of laughs and excitement. More to the point, you could earn money and save it at the same time. What I noticed was that every time Kenny came home on leave, he was more suntanned and far better off financially. I was like a headless chicken for the next few weeks and I must have spent more time at home with my family then, than at any other time. My father, who was excited for me, had been at sea himself for a

Pete Mitchell *alias* Stratmaster

few years during the Second World War. He had often told me about his escapades, and how he was washed overboard more than once. He was out on the Atlantic convoys, doing escort duties for the merchant ships. Apparently, the sea around the Scapa Flow area is supposed to be one of the roughest stretches of water in the world. My father would always finish the conversation with an encouraging word, reassuring me that modern ships were far safer now, and that the Merchant Navy always had an excellent record for safety. Just as well, considering I was about to climb aboard one of their super safe vessels, and put my life in their hands. To be honest, I had a feeling of excitement, but I was still very nervous as to whether I had made the right decision.

Three weeks later my papers came through, and I folded up the band that I was with. My cases were packed, but more importantly, my guitar was ready for action. The instructions from P&O were to leave within a few days and go to Tilbury docks. Berthed there was the P&O ship, 'Arcadia'. On board, I was to meet the chief steward, who would eventually show me to my cabin. Later, I was to find out that I wouldn't be sailing on this ship. They had only sent me there as a stand-by, and the whole crew had reported back for duty. The next morning, after spending my first night on board in a luxury cabin, I was woken up by the chief steward. He promptly told me that he would not need my services, but if I went down below to the galley, (ship's kitchen) I could help myself to some breakfast.

After trudging all the way to Kent like a packhorse, with the view to sailing off into the sunset the next day on the 'Arcadia', only to disembark and trek all the way back home, I was not amused. One feels a bit of an idiot saying good-bye to everyone, telling them that you'll write to them in three month's time, only suddenly having to explain why you are back there twenty-four hours later. Anyway, everyone seemed

OUTSIDE LOOKING IN

to be very understanding, and within a few weeks, I received another set of orders from P&O. This time, they told me to go to Southampton docks and board the 'Oriana', which was berthed there. I was to report to the chief steward with my rating of 'Utility Steward'. After my last experience on board the 'Arcadia', which, incidentally, was due to go out of service at any time, I was naturally very delighted to find myself on board the beautiful, modern 'Oriana'. There was absolutely no comparison between 'Arcadia' and 'Oriana'. 'Arcadia' had twelve crew members to a cabin, and 'Oriana' had only two per cabin. 'Oriana' was, in fact, the second newest ship in the fleet and weighed 42,000 tons. The newest ship was the flagship 'Canberra'.

The modem cruise liner was a real eye-opener for me. I had never been on board anything like it before. In fact, the closest I had ever been was a ride on the Mersey ferry. I was about fourteen years old, and went to Liverpool to see my grandmother on my mother's side. I went down to the docks on my own and boarded the ferry to New Brighton. I remember that day vividly. It was the first time that I had traveled on a boat by myself, and I had the feeling I was sailing off around the world. Just the smell of the sea air and the noise from the gulls was enough to stimulate my schoolboy imagination and fascination for the sea. The ocean-going liner was really something else. I hadn't realised just how huge they were, and that inside they were built with all the facilities and luxuries you could possibly imagine. There were heated pools on deck, ballrooms, theatres, bars, restaurants, games rooms and hospitals with daily surgery. Passenger accommodation was superb, and so were the crew quarters. My living quarters were excellent, and we had our own baths and showers available. Such incredible engineering, and I was very keen to be part of the 'Oriana' crew. This ship was actually a floating city, with absolutely everything you could possibly want on board.

Pete Mitchell *alias* Stratmaster

This time, I was accepted and signed on in the ship's logbook. To be honest, I was just relieved to get on board and settle into my cabin. I knew that very soon I would be sailing to the other side of the world on a very comfortable ship, with exceptional food on the menu, and, more to the point, getting paid to travel. All I needed now was a good night's sleep. The next day, I would get a plan of action drawn up regarding a band. I knew, by talking to friends, that there would be plenty of free time at sea and that the social life on board would be electric. My intentions were to capitalize on this and play whenever and however I could. I got into the swing of things very quickly on board 'Oriana'. It was quite a natural adjustment and before long, I was feeling like an old hand. My first job as a 'Utility Steward' was the first rung on the catering ladder.

I had to report for duty at seven o'clock every morning, for seven days a week, and get out the mops and buckets. I was part of what was known as the 'Chain Gang'. It was our job to clean the ship from bow to stem and be responsible for the basic hygiene throughout the ship. There were forms of promotion within the different departments, and after a while, you would be taken off the loo cleaning and be given an electric floor polisher. If you were given one of those, you knew that you were moving up the ladder slightly. You realised how big the ship was when you had to polish every square inch of the decks. It could take all morning to wax and polish just one of them. This was a never-ending task, and it became one more mechanical process.

Every few weeks, there would be a change of role, and some of us would go down below to work in the stores. Every time the ship docked, local produce would be taken on board and, by doing this, there would always be a supply of fresh food available. We would take on apples from Cape Town, lamb from New Zealand, Bacardi from Nassau and so on. There is nothing quite like the taste of a fresh coconut or pineapple when it has just been cut. Working with the stores meant hours of physical exercise. When you are loading hundreds of lamb, tons of vegetables, and hundreds of gallons of milk, you sleep very well at night. The volume of food consumed on one trip ran into tons, and the stores that came aboard included many other items. Everything had to be checked and stored, and most of it had to be kept in cold rooms and refrigerated. On every trip, tons of baggage would be loaded and unloaded. This was a continuous activity from port to port, and we would usually finish working around seven o'clock that evening.

Eventually, I was promoted. The next rung up the ladder was to 'Assistant Steward'. There were various stewards throughout the ship, ranging from waiters to bedroom stewards, from wine stewards to public room stewards. All these people had specific jobs to do, and their sole purpose was to look after the passengers' interests. If anything was needed, like an aspirin, or shoes and clothes to be washed and cleaned at any time, day or night, the stewards were there to take care of it. All the tables in the restaurants were laid up before each meal, and every passenger waited on hand and foot. The wine waiter would keep the wines at the right temperature and make sure that his customers' glasses were always full. I have never seen such a massive operation run with such precision to such a high standard in any other business.

My promotion came as a waiter, and I reluctantly accepted the offer, as it was never a good idea to refuse it. We all knew that if you did, it would be a long wait before you got another chance. I suddenly realised that I had been thrown into the deep end, for my waiting skills were rather limited. It meant that I would have to come into contact directly with the

Pete Mitchell *alias* Stratmaster

passengers, serve them their meals and generally make a fuss of them, even if they were rude or bad tempered. I have to say that I was very uncomfortable in this particular job, and I realised that I was not cut out for it. I was definitely not put on this earth to serve and wait on people. After a very embarrassing bangers and mash spillage, right into the lap of an irate passenger, who, in my opinion, asked for it, I felt that I had all the justification needed to quit. I was quickly moved back onto the 'Chain Gang', where I stayed for a few more months. I was pleased with the transfer at this point because it gave me a lot more free time, which enabled me to work more with the band. I eventually gained favour and got my promotion for the second time to 'Leading Hands Mess Man'. It sounds complicated, but it was a brilliant job, and was so good that I kept it throughout the rest of my service. The job entailed running the officers' mess and managing their meal times. It was a bit like running your own cafe.

The great thing about the Merchant Navy is that you meet all kinds of characters. You have to get on together, and you all have similar goals, basically, to have a good time, work hard and earn the money. All the lads were similar to me, coming from poor backgrounds, and most of them had never been abroad before. I have to say, in hindsight, that I did meet a lot of down to earth guys in the Merchant Navy. There was a genuine feel about them, a kind of brotherly quality. Once again, I realised that one of the best things around for breaking the ice was the guitar. It never failed me. I only needed to play a few tunes and I would notice a positive reaction, with a feeling of respect and appreciation. We had countless parties and singsongs, and I wanted to take the music one step further.

After a few weeks at sea, I started to miss my band from England. By talking to some of the lads, I was able to express my frustrations and able to find out who was musical.

OUTSIDE LOOKING IN

Normally, there is never a shortage of guitar players, and so I decided to start the search. I started to find out who played what and who wanted to sing. Everyone was keen to join the band, and as it stood, the band could have easily consisted of some twenty members. As enthusiasm was not enough, I short-listed the suitable volunteers. The band comprised myself on guitar and vocals, Peter, an ex-policeman from Wembly who was learning bass, and Jonah, a young lad from Devon, who was obsessed with the drums, but unfortunately didn't own any. On second guitar, we had Dave, from Leeds, who knew enough chords to make a promising start. There were a few volunteers to sing, but with all the work we had to do musically, we didn't need to worry about the vocals. Meetings and chats took place frequently. In between shifts and port visits, we would arrange practices. I was giving the bass player ongoing lessons and within a few weeks, we had a rhythm section (except drums) playing reasonably well. We scraped together a dozen songs and gradually progressed to an acceptable standard. Now I was very involved, and I started to get offers to play at social events and parties aboard. After some discussion, a far more serious plan emerged, and we agreed unanimously to develop the band.

On arrival in Vancouver, we bought a drum kit for Jonah, some new amplifiers and guitars, complete with a P/A system (public address system). By the time we sailed on our second trip to Australia, we had a presentable act. We needed to polish up a few things, but we were playing and having fun, and that, for me, was all that mattered. The band was named the 'Shades of Blue'. We played at the captain's party, passengers' parties, and regularly for the crew. Later, we played at a dance where the highlight of the evening was being in the company of Hayley Mills. She was on board filming 'Pretty Polly'. Gigs would often be pre-arranged with passengers, who wanted to celebrate their anniversaries and weddings.

Pete Mitchell *alias* Stratmaster

Most of the time at sea was spent working, or, as in my case, playing with the band. A lot of the time was spent traveling, and all the social activity was on board. Mind you, when we docked into port and went ashore, it was a very different matter altogether. As a teenager, I was very familiar with the pubs, and even more familiar with the beer inside. I was about fifteen years old and definitely under age when I remember being out with my father and drinking my first pint in a pub. How can you forget such a moment? I was hiding under the table in the saloon bar, keeping out of sight from the adults, while happily drinking my stout. Of course, one thing led to another over the years, and now I like to think that I have mastered the art of drinking. My teenage apprenticeship in drinking certainly stood me in good stead for the Navy. Just when you thought you'd seen it all with big drinkers, you were suddenly educated one step further. When going ashore with these guys, you had a very different experience. You would always get the odd idiot who would end up flat out and dead to the world, but generally speaking, the majority of these lads would go ashore for the evening and drink themselves stupid. They would swallow gallons of beer and all kinds of drinks, and yet they would still hold a decent conversation with you. Truly amazing. I put it down to state of mind and hours of practice. I hate to think what it did to their livers, but they certainly put it away, only to be ready the next morning for work. I can remember going ashore in Japan, where we decided to go to a club in Yokohama. Six of us sat around the table, talking and drinking until midnight. There was a discussion going on, and we were trying to reach a decision as to whether we would go or stay. Eventually, we decided to stay, and all six of us sat at that table all night. We actually drank ourselves sober into the next morning. To my surprise, we left the club on foot and walked back to the ship, ready for breakfast and early duty. I still don't know to this day, how much money was spent on that binge.

OUTSIDE LOOKING IN

One of the most significant events to take place while I was in the Navy was the 'Hippie Explosion' that happened in America in 1967. It happened in San Francisco, and both musically and philosophically, this event had a major impact on me. Fortunately for me, as a young guy from Battersea, I was able to absorb this experience with the other members of my band. The whole city of San Francisco was paralysed by this phenomenon. I remember running around and being part of a twenty-four hour street party. Everyone I saw and spoke to seemed to be on cloud nine, and there were flowers everywhere. This was, without doubt, a real marker in time for my life. It wasn't until I'd seen this huge city, taken over by the Hippies with all-day roof parties and all-night love-ins, that I realised just how powerful this cocktail of youth, love, hope, faith and the desperate need for peace could be.

Having already seen San Francisco previously in its normal everyday routine, I certainly noticed the difference this time around. San Francisco had its cable cars and steep roads. The trams would reach the terminus at the end of the line, where they would turn them round on a turntable manually. Most of the houses were built on steep hills and designed beautifully. The shops were incredible, and down on Fisherman's Wharf they had just about every single sea creature you could think of. All the seafood was fresh, the restaurants served anything from crab and lobster, to tuna and conger eel. They were selling fish that I'd never heard of before. Fish like red snapper and hammerhead' shark.

In the record stores, they had thousands of albums by American artists who had never been heard of in England. These were mainly records that you couldn't buy in the United Kingdom because they were never exported from America. I knew that this would eventually change, and within twelve months, they were flooding the British market with albums recorded by American artistes. On seeing this great city with the Hippie occupation, you would never have believed that it was the same place. Even the Golden Gate Park was swamped with joint smoking Hippies and psychedelic freaks. Streets were blocked off, with thousands of ordinary people dressing up and dropping out. Some were just plain weekend Hippies. I couldn't comprehend it, then it hit me in the face like a hammer. I had seen nothing like it before, it was not until I got back to England that I was able to find out about it and try to understand what had happened.

Later, I would witness the effect of its cultural impact. I had never seen so much colour and excitement before, particularly on such a massive scale. Whenever I hear the 'Hippie Anthem' (If You Are Going To San Francisco by Scott McKensie), it reminds me of the first time I sailed into San Francisco harbour. We were sailing directly under the Golden Gate Bridge as the song was blaring out of our transistor radios. I get that same feeling, a kind of nostalgic action replay in my head, every time I hear that song. On my return from San Francisco, I brought back an album by a band that was unknown in England at that time. For me, this band personified this event with their music and philosophy. This incredible band was none other than the 'Doors', and I think the name says it all. Their album was called, 'Morrison Hotel' and the lead singer was called Jim Morrison.

My thirst to travel was finally quenched. There were a lot of good times had with the 'Shades of Blue', both on stage and off, and I must have traveled around the world a dozen times over. I never got blasé about it, because every trip was different. I visited Hawaii many times and it was there that I managed to get my first taste of surfing. This was something completely new to me. I had never seen anyone surf before. Let's face it; there are very few places around the English coast that are suitable for this. Rarely do we get the right weather, and the sea is hardly that inviting. Between oil slicks, sewage, shipping lanes, and a continual lack of the sun, we don't have a chance of competing with places like California, Waikiki, and Bondi. These are all fabulous surfing beaches, with golden sands and crystal-clear, blue seas. I used to watch the surfers in California. Some of them were just young kids who were riding these huge waves. It was such an impressive sight, especially when they went out and surfed the 'pipeline'. This was considered the ultimate achievement of any surfer. Apparently, some of the surfers attempting this feat have drowned.

The 'pipeline' is a huge roller wave that goes up to thirty or forty feet high and then it wraps itself around you, and you have to surf along it as if you were gliding down a long tube. One slip and you were in serious trouble, mainly because of the vast expanse of water and pressure that built up. If it collapsed, you could very easily drown. There were always instructors on the beaches who would give advice and lessons to beginners. Even more noticeable were the lifeguards, especially on the Australian beaches. I started to learn how to surf myself, but very quickly realised how difficult it was. As a kid I used to roller skate and I spent hours in the swimming baths. I loved the water, but surfing was something else. My first attempt at it proved to be rather a failure.

After managing to get out with the board into the surf, the next step was to stand up on it and catch the crest of the next wave. It's all about balance and timing, and, like any other sport, you have to spend time getting into the techniques of it. After a while, I got up onto the board, only to be thrown about ten feet into the air. I went under the water and the surfboard came down on top of me. I felt an enormous smash and it turned out that the centre fin on the surfboard had hit my head hard and gashed a nasty two-inch cut. When I opened

Pete Mitchell *alias* Stratmaster

my eyes, the water around me was red, and I knew immediately that I had become a victim of this incredibly challenging sport. Luckily, I was able to go straight to the first aid post on the beach and have it stitched up. So much for surfing.

I remember visiting Hawaii on one occasion and, by chance, I bumped into Mike Love. He was a very respected member of the 'Beach Boys', and was on vacation in Honolulu. We were introduced and I had a very interesting conversation with him. He told me how much he liked England, and I mentioned that I had seen him with his band six months earlier, at their concert in Tooting, London. This amused him and we had a beer together. I couldn't think of a better way to spend an afternoon then chatting with a superstar and drinking cold beer on the beautiful and exotic island of Hawaii.

CHAPTER 3
MEDITERRANEAN MADNESS

After some two years of sailing around the world seeing paradise islands and visiting just about every country with a port, I was starting to get restless once again. I was actually getting fed up with the constant traveling, and the boys in the 'Shades of Blue' were also thinking of doing other things. None of us expected to stay in the Navy too long. That probably would have been the kiss of death for most of us and I think it would have led to the majority of the lads becoming alcoholics. We all knew that we would only work at sea for a couple of years and then we would move on. It must be said, that while at sea I did experience another side to the Navy, and it wasn't all rosy. After witnessing the death of a good friend at sea and having to sail through hurricane 'Flossie', with forty-foot waves tossing you around like a cork, I realised that there were serious risks involved. Very scary, I'd say, knowing full well that there were not enough life boats to go round should the ship go down. It was a known fact that apart from the captain, the crew would be the last ones to leave the ship. The funny thing was, I was far more concerned about my guitar.

Pete Mitchell *alias* Stratmaster

I had kept in constant touch with my girlfriend throughout my time at sea, and she wrote to me regularly at every port. I would answer as often as I could, and I must confess I was amazed that the letters were so regular. At the beginning, I used to think that they would probably slow down, or even stop. Now, I needed to get back home and sort out my so-called relationship. It didn't quite have the same appeal to me anymore, because I wasn't ready to settle down and I had discovered that my girlfriend was gay. Finding out that my future wife was bisexual was, sadly, the final nail in the coffin lid. This was my exit from any serious relationship that I might have had. I decided to sign off 'Oriana', and collect my wages due.

I remember heading back home to Beclands and having a two-week nonstop binge, spending money as if it was the end of the world. In my last letter from home, having followed me around the world, my sister told me that my younger brother, John, had been born. This came as quite a shock to me, in view of the fact I was twenty-two and my sister was twenty-three. I was pleased to be back home. I just wanted to relax and catch up with my music career.

It was the summer of 1968 and I decided to visit a good friend of mine in Battersea. His name was Chris, and I had grown up with him as a teenager. We both decided that it was time to have a good laugh and go abroad for a while. Chris had been telling me all along that getting married wasn't for me, that if I did, I would be finished. Chris and I had been through some tough times together as teenagers, and he was probably my first serious drinking partner. He was keen on playing the guitar, and over the years I had taught him enough to amuse himself. Like Jimmy and myself, he was a Battersea lad through and through. We had many a drink together in the 'Long Bar' on Waterloo Station, usually after an all-night session in a Soho club. Chris lived with his grandmother, as his father died when he was very young. He jumped off of Chelsea Bridge trying to save someone from drowning. Chris was told years later that his father had drowned with the person he was saving. I think there is a moral there somewhere. I know this had quite an effect on Chris, and he often talked about it.

We eventually planned to go to Spain for the summer, and I drew out some money from the bank. We stayed at his grandmother's house that evening and decided to have an early night. We knew that we would have to get up early the next morning, because we were leaving for France. We got up at about seven and started to sort things out. There was a beautiful smell of fried bacon and tomatoes wafting through the flat, and I could hear the bacon sizzling in the kitchen. His grandmother was convinced that we would both need a king-size breakfast, and admitted that she was very concerned about our welfare and when were we coming back to England. She said that if we wanted some fried bread with our breakfast, we would have to tell her a lot more about our plans. The point was, neither of us knew the answer to that question, for the whole object of this exercise was to get away and play the whole thing by ear. We said we would be away for about six weeks, which, in fact, turned out to be almost nine months. With cases packed and stomachs full, we decided it was time to leave. After a few tears and good-byes, we set off for Waterloo Station, and, to be perfectly honest; we couldn't wait to get out of Battersea.

We caught the train to Dover and crossed the channel on the ferry. With both of us sampling the duty-free spirits on the boat, we arrived in rather a merry state. It was on this occasion that I realised that the French police disliked us coming to France. They hated long hair, and having the acoustic guitar with us didn't help matters either. They weren't very happy with the threat of us busking. I think we were considered

Pete Mitchell *alias* Stratmaster

Hippies and dropouts. Having left Calais, we found ourselves walking along in the middle of nowhere, and eventually we came across a cafe. We were invited in and made very welcome. Yes, you have guessed it, they noticed my guitar and wanted me to play some Beatle songs. This went on for the rest of the evening. As long as I played, they poured the wine. Eventually, we dropped from exhaustion and bedded down in a stable full of cattle. Early next morning, after having spent our first night in France, I woke up with a lousy hangover, feeling as if I had been beaten up. This was going to be the last time that I would allow myself to get so drunk, especially on cheap French plonk. Even with my naval training in the drinks department, I still suffered.

Now, in the true sense of the word, we were 'on the road'. Chris and I had limited funds, and part of the plan was to make our money last as long as humanly possible. Our destination was a small coastal town called Estartit, situated on the northeast coast of Spain. We knew that we had to travel south across France and then over the Spanish border to get to Estartit. Friends had told us that Estartit was a great place, that it wasn't a commercial town full of tourists. We had trekked some fifty kilometres and were heading towards Paris, having spent two long nights on the road. We had slept rough, and not eaten any decent food since leaving home. We caught a train to Paris and then changed onto the main line, which took us south to Narbonne, where we arrived late that evening.

We managed to get some food on the train, and there were plenty of cold beers available. After sleeping for a while, I was approached by a ticket inspector who told us to leave the train at the next station. This was due to the fact that we were in the wrong carriage. He said that our tickets were second-class, and that we were sleeping in a first-class compartment. Having

OUTSIDE LOOKING IN

been rumbled, we jumped off the train at the next stop, and moved further along the carriage. As soon as the coast was clear, we climbed back into a second-class compartment. No way were we going to be left in the middle of nowhere in a foreign country, unable to speak the language. After a bit more hounding, the same inspector decided to leave us alone, and we eventually arrived in Narbonne. There were no trains running until the next morning, so we had to bed down on the platform and wait for our connecting train the following morning. Much to our relief, the train arrived on time and we boarded it for the town of Gerona.

We arrived in Gerona at midday, and we went through the customs without any difficulty. Fortunately, we had enough money on us, and our papers and passports were in order. We were told later that Spanish Customs were strict with foreigners who entered Spain without sufficient finance. The last thing they wanted were droves of foreign, penniless Hippies flooding in at the locals' expense. They were having a problem with their economy, so I had to agree with their point of view. That afternoon, we arrived in Estartit, and sure enough, it was a beautiful village, exactly as they had described it.

Both of us knew that we were going to spend some time there, and needed to get sorted out and cleaned up as soon as possible. Unfortunately, I was rather badly sun burnt across the top of my shoulders, and needed to find a chemist and get some cream quickly. There were shops in the village, and I was able to sort this out without too much trouble. We roughed it for a few days, and then we met some English guys who were renting a house in Estartit. They said we could stay there for the night with them. By this time, we were feeling pretty exhausted, so we took up their offer and slept solidly for twenty-four hours. We had in fact overstayed our welcome, but the lads living there were cool about it. As we got to know them, they became more trusting and I think we ended up staying there for about a month. So far, we had been living on my savings, and we were both trying to find a way of earning some money. Within the first month, we had more or less sussed out the town, the people, and the opportunities. If we wanted to stay, we knew that we would have to earn a lot more money. I still had some cash at home, but that was allocated for an emergency or for our return fare home should we end up broke and destitute.

On the far side of the bay, there was a club called 'Custard Beast'. It was situated inside one of the main hotels and was to become a very significant place. We had to be members of the club, and in doing so; we made useful connections. We were able to make friends and meet lots of people, and some of the tourists would let us stay in their apartments for a while. The club gave us jobs and accommodation, and we became friends with the club owner. There were endless invitations to parties, with both him and his friends, and this made life a lot easier all round. In the town, there was a nice cafe bar, and this was the central meeting place.

We were meeting people from all over Europe here, as well as English tourists. Everyday there were boat trips around the islands and thirty or forty people would buy tickets for the barbecue. My job was to play guitar and entertain them throughout the trip. On board we would have cases of wine and stacks of chickens and burgers. Chris and I worked on these boats for a while, making some money and having a fabulous time. It was all about meeting people, entertaining them, and giving them a beach barbecue that they would never forget. I remember being drunk on one occasion and dropping a full magnum of Champagne on my foot. At the time, I didn't feel a thing but, the next day, I couldn't walk and ended up on crutches. A few weeks later, we happened to be hanging around the beach, where I was playing a few songs on the guitar. A guy in his late forties came along and stopped to listen. He was extremely well dressed, and introduced himself as Bob Miles. He said that he was having a party later that evening, and that if I agreed to play a few songs for him, we could both go. I have to say, we did wonder about this guy for a while, but in the end we decided to take him up on his offer. We found his house and boy, what a place! The house was packed, and I couldn't help but notice the two very attractive ladies sitting on either side of him. Sure enough, the corks were popping, drinks were flowing, and food was in abundance.

I knew that there had to be a catch, and halfway through the evening, Bob Miles asked me to play. The song he requested was 'Hey Jude', by the 'Beatles'. This song was being played all over Europe at that time. As soon as I started playing, everybody joined in, and it sounded as if we were in the middle of a Wembly cup match. How the roof stayed on, I will never know.

This was a great way to meet everyone, and Bob was a decent guy. He was very wealthy, very cool, and very kind. He gave us somewhere to live, rent free, for a few months, with lots of food and wine. We went to many more parties with him and his friends. Occasionally, he would take us out to dinner, still escorting a beautiful girl on his arm. Bob would always have a pretty girl with him, and when I asked him outright, 'Why are you so kind to us?' he said, 'I like you guys, you are genuine and I have the greatest respect for musicians'. Many times he said, 'Peter, never stop playing, and don't let anyone change your mind about your direction'. Bob was an Englishman who had his business in Germany. He also had other activities around the world. We found out later that he owned the diving club in Estartit, and that he went there regularly for his holidays. It was a very good business to have in a town like Estartit, especially when the whole scene centred on the beach and bay. Now and then, we would go diving with Bob and see the underwater caves. He said he loved to be among young people, and that we made him feel young. I asked him what his favourite pastime was, and he told me that one of them was listening to the guitar. On hearing this, I realised once again it was the guitar that held the attraction.

At weekends, we would usually go to the club and meet up with friends. I met a French girl there called Anne, who came from a wealthy family in Paris, and she spoke perfect English. Just as well really, as I couldn't speak much French at all. I stayed for a while with her at her apartment, while Chris was seeing an English girl from Surrey who had gone to Estartit for her summer holidays. Chris introduced us briefly, and, within a few days, she went back home to England. Anne was a sweet girl and a bit of a flirt, but we had some fun together. She said to me before she went back to Paris, 'I would like you to call in and visit me and my family on your way home to England'. I thanked her and said that I would bear it in mind, and if possible, we would. For about nine months, there was never a dull moment in Estartit.

Just as things started to slow down, something else came up. It was quite amazing when we arrived in Estartit, the Spanish police, who were also anti-Hippies, pestered us, and Chris was carted off and shut in a cell overnight. Some eight months later, we experienced a noticeable change in their attitude to the exact opposite. Chris and I were drinking in a bar where we were introduced to a Portuguese lad. He spoke good English and he had a good sense of humour. His name was Philippe, and, unknown to us, he had an uncle in high office on the Barcelona council. When we told him how the police had treated us in the earlier months, he was quite upset. We said we were harassed regularly on the beach, and that we had been raided late at night and threatened with guns. Philippe said that he was going to Barcelona for a while, and that he would see us when he came back.

Strangely, we noticed that the police chief and his cronies had become friendlier towards us, and couldn't do enough for us. We were now allowed to drink after hours in the bars and they were even buying us drinks. When Philippe returned, we mentioned this sudden change of attitude to him. He said that he had spoken to his uncle, and that his uncle had told him he would sort the matter out immediately. This was a perfect example of 'it's not what you know, but who you know'. Having had a superb time in Spain, we were ready to start thinking about getting back home and checking out the music scene. Friends threw a party for us on our last night in Estartit, and we said our good-byes and farewells, knowing that we might never see them again.... Such is life.

We drank until the early hours, and later that day we got a lift from Estartit to the Spanish border. Our friends knew that we were broke and that we had a long journey ahead of us. They gave us enough money to buy a couple of meals. Once we crossed the border, however, the real ordeal started. As we headed further north, we could feel the weather turning much colder. We were hitchhiking from the border, without much luck, walking for hours. After walking about ten kilometres, we met a young French girl on the road. She was hitchhiking back to her hometown of Toulouse. She said that the only way we would get a lift would be to trick the drivers into stopping for us. The game was simple. We had to hide out of sight behind the bushes while she thumbed the trucks down. When the driver pulled up, she would climb in, while we were to be quick and jump up into the cab with her. By the time the driver realised what was going on, all three of us would be in the cab, and that was that. I think it's called the element of surprise. Chris and I got this off to a fine art, especially when we realised that this was the only way of getting back home successfully. We arrived in Toulouse and sadly left our sweet lady companion. Now we were on our own, with some seven hundred miles to go before reaching Calais.

For three days, we hitchhiked and walked from Toulouse, making very little progress. We were very hungry and slowly becoming disillusioned with French hospitality when suddenly, our prayers were answered. A couple of students stopped for us in a Citroen 2CV. We were so tired and exhausted when we got into the car, that we slept for twelve hours. When we eventually woke up, we had reached the outskirts of Paris. I thanked the students for our lift, and we started to make our way across Paris in a northerly direction. By this time, we were near to starvation, having spent what little money we had. Sadly, my Gibson guitar had been stolen in Spain, so I couldn't even busk and earn some money for food. Things were desperate, when I suddenly remembered the invitation I had from Anne! She had asked us to call in and see her with her family in Paris when traveling back home to England. Paris is a huge city, especially when you are tired and hungry. We eventually found Anne's flat, which was in a very exclusive suburb of Paris. The main door had a security phone, and inside there was a porter on duty. We managed to attract his attention, but he seemed reluctant to open the door to us. I wasn't surprised, because we must have looked like a couple of real 'down and outs'. We were standing in our bare feet, unshaven, with no decent clothes, having just spent the last five days surviving on the road. Intrigued, the porter opened the door, and we managed to tell him why we were there.

OUTSIDE LOOKING IN

I gave him the slip of paper that Anne had written the address on, and he looked at it and walked over to the intercom. I assumed that he phoned up to the flat, to inform the lucky residents that they had visitors. Someone answered the phone, and we waited for Anne to appear. We were hoping she would come down and invite us up to her apartment for a hot bath and a decent meal. The porter sent us up to the fifth floor and we rang the doorbell. A butler opened the door and stared in horror. He took one look at us and went back inside. I could see that there was a dinner party under way, and the guests were all dressed up in dinner suits. A smartly dressed guy who looked about fifty came to the door and said in broken English, 'Anne is not here'.

Can you imagine how we felt? There we were, starving to death in the middle of Paris, and we told to go away. Chris and I left the building totally dejected. For the first time, I was seriously worried about getting back home.

We roamed around for a while until we came across a safe house. This was a home for waifs and strays. In the foyer, hanging on the wall, was a picture in a beautiful, gilded frame of a tramp. I thought, at last, we would be fed and, if we were very lucky, we might even get a bed for the night. Not so. We were told that we couldn't stay there because we were too scruffy and didn't have any money. Can you believe that? Just as we were about to leave, a young lady came over to me and said she was disturbed by our plight. She was a social worker and she spoke fluent English. She said she felt obliged to help us. She lived with her father in a flat nearby, and wanted us to go back with her for an evening meal, a hot bath and a clean up. All of what we didn't get from Anne. It seemed like a miracle with this total stranger giving us not only her time, but also sharing her home with us. After a good clean up, we went into the dining room. Her father was sitting at the table in a wheelchair placed at one end. He was extremely friendly towards us and later in the conversation, he said that he had a lot of respect for the English. This was his way of thanking us for the kindness shown by the British troops when Paris was liberated in 1945 during the Second World War. We had a very pleasant evening, with excellent food and wine, and we thanked them both for their hospitality. We were both shattered, and after a comfortable night's sleep on the camp bed, we got up and had some breakfast. They gave us some money to get across Paris, and we were starting to feel like human beings again.

We got on the Metro train and crossed Paris, starting out on the last stretch of the journey to Calais. Feeling refreshed with a full stomach, we continued to hitchhike home. In France, hitchhiking wasn't acceptable, and was considered by most people to be illegal, especially if you were English travelers and Hippies. Later, we got a lift from a farmer who appeared to be taking his milk to early morning market. He only took us a few kilometres, but it still boosted our morale. The weather was getting colder and we had very few clothes. To make it worse, it poured with rain. At this point, I think we had about two hundred miles to go and we were walking endlessly. Chris still had his old shoes, but I was bare footed, as my shoes were worn out, plus my jeans were only just holding together. After walking a few more kilometres, we decided to look for some shelter so that we could rest and get some sleep.

We spent the night sleeping in a garage, as the door had been left open. We were sound asleep when suddenly I heard a car engine. I woke up to see the back end of a truck reversing into us. When we realised what was happening, we shot out of the garage, the driver nearly died of shock. He obviously didn't know that we were in there sleeping until he heard us choking on the exhaust fumes. We were very cold, and because we had no money, we were unable to buy any food. We were eating raw vegetables from the gardens and the occasional corn on the cob from the fields. Having tramped for two more days, we were becoming more and more demoralized by the hour. Stuck in the middle of nowhere at midnight, with the rain teeming down with empty stomachs really wasn't a good position to be in. By pure chance, I noticed a shadow in the middle of a field, which turned out to be a haystack.

I said to Chris, 'We don't have any choice mate, either we get inside it, or we'll both freeze to death'.

Chris was very close to tears; the bitter cold and relentless rain had gotten to him. He was at a breaking point, so I ripped out the middle of the haystack and we climbed in. I kept him as warm as I could, and we managed to sleep for a couple of hours. I tried to raise his spirits up by talking about getting home, and this seemed to be working.

We pulled ourselves together and set off back on the road with the rain still pouring and no sign of a change in the weather. Within half an hour, we got a lift from a guy who was driving to Calais. He told us that he was a French journalist on his way to England on business. I think he must have realised how hungry we were, for after travelling a few kilometres, he stopped at a cafe. As luck would have it, he bought us coffee with bread and cheese. We had reached the end of an incredible journey, and what a way to finish our ordeal. We finally arrived in Calais, and I never thought I could be so excited just with seeing the ferry. Chris and I had spent six days and nights on the road with no money, and we had travelled over eight hundred miles.

CHAPTER 4
BITING THE BULLET

On August 9th, 1969, I got married. My wife Jenny was eighteen years old and I was twenty-three. In retrospect, this was rather a quick and sudden affair. We met originally in Spain, and I saw her again about six months later, in England. I happened to be drinking in a bar in Richmond, when to my surprise, who should walk in but Jenny. I was actually living at my grandmother's house in Battersea, and I had the top flat. I worked in the house for a few months and completely refurbished the top floor. My grandmother seemed to be pleased with me living there, but I got very bored after a while and realised that this situation was not going to work out.

I was seeing Jenny, who lived in Byfleet, a small village in Surrey. She would come up to London and see me two or three times a week and gradually, we got more involved. Before long, we were talking about settling down and getting married. There were two reasons for this sudden decision, and the first one was rather delicate. I knew that my grandmother wasn't too keen on me getting married. I think she was getting a little possessive in her old age, but she was a sweet old lady who was very kind and very disciplined. She came from the old Victorian school, had worked hard all her life and saved a little bit for a rainy day. The point was she did not want me to bring girls back home, so I would have to leave and find myself a place. The second reason for getting out was that I felt ready to share a home and live with someone. What I intended to do was rent a furnished flat for a while, with the intention of getting an unfurnished flat at a later date. We had a registry office wedding and lived for a while in a furnished flat in Kingston Upon Thames. Twelve months later, we moved into an unfurnished flat in Surbiton. Fortunately for us, it was the perfect place. It was a large flat in a beautiful Victorian detached house.

Up until now, I had been playing on and off with bands and jamming with friends. It was high time to get down to it and put a new band together. I had been promising myself for a while that I would buy a really nice old guitar. The one I had in mind was an old Fender 'Telecaster'. I noticed an advertisement in the Melody Maker for a music shop in Putney that had an original 'Telecaster' for sale. Having managed to scrape together the two hundred pounds needed to buy it, I went over to the shop to have a look. Well, the moment I saw it, that was it. The body was a natural finish, and it turned out to be a 1953 original. What made it even more unique was the 1954 Stratocaster maple neck that was on it. Looking back, I think it was probably one of the best guitars I have ever owned. I still wonder to this day whether the shop knew what its real value was. A few weeks later, when coming out of the job centre, I met an old musician friend of mine. His name was John Presley, and we were always scratching about together, trying to make ends meet. John was a good bass player and singer, a true 'rock and roller'. He left his band, called 'Madding Crowd', and formed a new one with me. This had been on the cards for some time.

Pete Mitchell *alias* Stratmaster

I worked well with John. We had a similar attitude towards the music and we had great respect for each other as musicians. We didn't agree on everything, but I think it was probably the first time that I actually appreciated the benefits of playing regularly with someone. It was important to use each other to bounce ideas back and forth, like a sounding board. John had been writing for a few years and managed to get a couple of songs published. Looking back, I know that he gave me a lot of valuable advice about the music business, and influenced me a great deal. From then on, I really wanted to develop my writing, and this proved to be a very productive working relationship. Both of us would spend weeks working on ideas for the band, trying to get the right songs. We could both sing, and that meant that the band could have two lead vocalists. Our song selection at the time included many blues tracks like Elmore James and BB King, crossed over with rock and roll tracks by Marti Wilde, Elvis, and Eddie Cochran. We were also playing our own original songs in the repertoire.

The idea behind this 'Blues and Rock fusion' was that I was a blues man at heart, and John was very much a rock and roller. We thought that this would be a very interesting combination, and we would end up with something bluesy, with a nice punchy rock feel. I can remember going to John's place and spending all day, and sometimes all night, playing and writing together. We would probably do this for a week or more, the only refreshments we'd have would be some crates of cider. We must have drunk gallons of the stuff between us, and I am sure we believed this was the vital ingredient to the success of writing hit material. Funny thing was, some good songs came out of it. The next day, we would play back the tapes that we had just recorded and often were pleasantly surprised.

OUTSIDE LOOKING IN

The new band was formed and we went into rehearsals for a few weeks. Soon after, we were out playing on the pub circuit. The band was called, 'Ambush' and I can remember playing a great gig in 1970 at the Ship Hotel, Weybridge. The real buzz was to see an advert in the press later, saying, 'top group, 'Ambush', returns after the great reception you gave them last month'. I have usually managed to earn some money with all the bands I've been with. I know the music comes first, but we still have to eat. By getting paid to play, we gain our respect. A musician without any pride might just as well stay in bed.

Around this same time, I remember going to the BBC studios in Maida Vale, where we were asked to play a live session. While we were recording a couple of songs, we could hear this incredible sound coming out of the studio next door. Later we were told it was Dave Edmunds, playing his hit, 'I Hear You Knocking'. Both John and I knew only too well that it was not enough just to have a good sound. If you were looking for a record deal, the most important thing was originality. Of course, this wasn't quite the same thing if you just wanted to play pub gigs.

Later on, John introduced me to a record producer in New Maiden, Surrey. His name was John Aster and he had released a few records at that time. I was able to do a few things with him and work on a couple of his projects through the sixties and seventies. This was invaluable experience for me, and I learnt a hell of a lot from John Aster, particularly with studio techniques and record production. John was certainly a perfectionist, but, at the same time, his attitude was if it sounds right, put it on tape. He had gained some experience from working with the BBC, and I found out later that the recording desk he was using was originally used at the BBC studios. This archaic piece of equipment, by today's standards, was incomparable. It was only a two-track machine, and all the instrumentation and backing tracks had to be recorded in one take. The reason being, the second track had to be used for the vocals. This meant there were no more tracks available for overdubbing extra instruments. The only way we could add further overdubs was to bounce the tracks across by using the tape machines. John had some good ideas and he would always find a way around the problem. It was terribly risky way to alter anything on the rhythm track, for, at a later stage, you wouldn't be able to. This meant that all recording had to be planned right down to the last detail. There were no facilities to layer track on track. It was a great experience for me to learn recording in this way. Because of this technical limitation, it forced us to get it right. Everyone noticed that nine times out of ten, you would have a spontaneous feel on the track. It was never too cluttered or over produced, as is often the case today. My only real gripe with that method was, if you had a great backing track down and suddenly heard a bum note or noise of some kind, you had to do it all over again. You couldn't pull that instrument out and re-record it again, while keeping the backing track. It's a hard life, especially when you realize that today most studios can offer a computerised sixty-four track desk anytime.

One of the best days of my life was 23rd November, 1970. My daughter Mishka was born, and on the night of her birth, I was playing at a gig. Mishka was always close to me as a child, and I like to think that she has been supportive throughout my career. I did manage to teach her some chords on the guitar when she was younger, and we did have some brilliant times together. They were precious moments and very special times.

After the birth, I spent the rest of that year working with 'Ambush' on the pub circuit in between changing nappies and decorating the flat in Surbiton. At that time, Habitat was in

OUTSIDE LOOKING IN

vogue, and I painted the whole flat using their colours. It was mulberry red and bilberry blue in the lounge, and lettuce green in the bathroom. They were great colours, so bright and fresh.

So far, I had. been slogging away on the pub circuits, and Jenny was expecting our second child. On 31st December, 1971 (New Year's Eve) my son Tyler was born. Quite a coincidence really, when you think that New Year's Eve is the most important gig of the year for any pub musician. This time I was hoping for a son, and I think most fathers do at some stage. Well, true to form, I was out at a New Year's Eve do when I heard the news. I was completely speechless, it was a dream come true. Jenny was a good mother, and nothing ever came before the kids. I found that as time went on, as long as there was enough money in the coffers for the things she wanted with the least amount of worries, things would probably tick along all right. In order to keep on playing and hold the fort at the same time, I had to sort out any problems.

Jenny knew how much the music meant to me, and she seemed to cope. A few ups and downs maybe, but that's the same for anyone in a family situation. Rarely did she come to gigs, but she used to like listening to the band occasionally at rehearsals. Often, I would put both carrycots into my minivan and then load up my gear and go off to rehearsals. Both of my kids grew up with the music, and it was second nature to them. There would be rock and roll playing at full volume, and both of them would sleep through it all. It was never a problem. Financial pressures would come up now and again, and I had to be flexible. When things got tight, it usually meant that I would have to sell some of my music gear. I can remember one time being behind with the rent and at the same time thinking, '*Oh God, here goes my Telecaster guitar*'.

Pete Mitchell *alias* Stratmaster

The problem was that this was my working guitar, and I had to sell it. My only consolation was that I knew it was going to a musician who would appreciate it. The lucky guy in question was none other than Mike Rutherford from 'Genesis'. The next day I spent suffering from severe shock. I did eventually get over it, as one usually does, but it took a while and I had to borrow another guitar immediately, because the band had to keep working. This business of making music was all about making sacrifices, and selling that guitar was like cutting one of my arms off.

CHAPTER 5
SOMETHING BREWING

Inside my head I could feel the pressure building up, with a highly explosive charge of emotion, anxiety, and determination spinning around at the same time. I knew that it was time to sit down and do some serious writing. I had new ideas for songs. In the early part of 1974, my philosophy and views on life, coupled with the passion for playing, demanded a new approach to my music. I felt that the most natural way to work would be with a twelve-string guitar. It would enable me to develop my acoustic technique, and I would be able to structure the new songs differently, writing them with stronger melodies. Rock and Roll songs tend to consist of two or three chords, a good example of this is the Blues, which has a very limited structure and framework when it comes to melody. I am very much a Blues man, and my roots are from the Blues and Rock and Roll. Influences through the sixties gave me a real interest in melodies.

One has to remember that a creative artiste who wants to record and release original material must be aware of the word 'commercialism', which really means originality. This doesn't necessarily mean originality in the sound or delivery, but it could depend on the image and the content. There has never been an art form, to my knowledge, that has depended so much on gimmicks and eccentricity as the so-called 'Pop World'. I am sure the word 'originality' has stuck in many a songwriter's throat, far more often than any fish bone.

Bearing all this in mind, it seemed quite natural for me to start writing on the twelve-string guitar, and so I did. I was fortunate enough to meet someone in the music business who had his own music shop in Kingston Upon Thames. He was an ex pro drummer who had worked with many of the big names in the early sixties like Joe Brown, Baron Knights, Unit 4+2, and so on. He introduced himself as Howard Conder, and we became good friends. Living close to his shop meant that I could have access to various instruments and equipment. I used a Tony Zemaitis twelve-string guitar for my main work and my Fender Telecaster (Circa 53) for ad work.

For about twelve months, I worked hard writing songs and I started to form my new band. I hoped that this one would be commercially successful, or, at least be out gigging full-time, though I knew that I would be happy whatever the outcome. Various players were selected, players who were musically competent, who respected me and rated the songs. I wanted people that would work with the material and have a good attitude towards it. I was excited about the possibility of working with these talented players, and even more excited with their potential. By being in the driving seat, I realised that there would be a few problems, and my job was going to be to control and harness the output. Songs were piling up, the band was rehearsing seriously, and there were signs of interest from the music business.

OUTSIDE LOOKING IN

Howard had a recording studio in Kingston Upon Thames, and we were able to rent part of it. This enabled us to knock the band into shape and to rehearse daily, if necessary. Having the gear set up and being able to walk in and out at any time was quite a luxury. All we had to do was switch on the mains and play. After a few weeks working hard at it, we were ready for the road. The fascinating thing about the music business is that it has to change its ideas and its image, and the fashion can't stay the same for too long. Of course, this is the last thing an artiste wants when he has just worked his backside off trying to get a deal. You've got specific ideas in mind when suddenly the whole scene changes, and you realise that, once again, you are going to miss the boat.

In the summer of 1974, after some careful thought, we named the band, 'Special Brew'. I chose the name myself, and people often asked me how the name originated. It arrived because of two reasons. Firstly, we were using different instruments compared to most of the bands at that time, and secondly, while writing the songs for the band's repertoire, I was drinking Special Brew lager. We were signed to 'Elephant Management' in Piccadilly and within weeks, we were out playing on the college circuit in the south of England. We played some good clubs, and one of the highlights was a show at the 'Chelsea Village' in Bournemouth with the Steve Gibbons band supporting us.

My favourite college was 'Kingston Polytechnic', and we gigged there a few times. I remember the last time we were there we had Jake Thackeray as a support act. He was a very funny man and extremely talented, and had been playing around the clubs for years. Jake had his own brand of music and wit, and we enjoyed his company. The band was getting anxious to record, and in order to make further progress, it needed to get a record deal. We spent a few days at the

Pete Mitchell *alias* Stratmaster

'Olympic Studios' in Barnes and recorded a batch of songs there. Most of them were self-penned, with ideas and input from the band. Pete McKerrow, who played keyboards, helped a great deal with the technical side of things. He was a trained pianist who could read and play almost anything by ear. Working with him was a privilege, and we had some fun. On bass, we had Geof Hammond, and, on lead guitar, we had Roger Giffin. At that time, Roger was building custom guitars for the rich and famous. Roger went on to work for 'Gibson' guitars in America, as head designer in their custom shop. On drums, we had Terry Threadingham, who came from the 'Magic Mushroom Band' in Portsmouth.

The songs were finally mixed and, after some skilful engineering and compromising, we had about thirteen master tracks recorded. Our engineer was Keith Harwood, who was responsible for some major hit records, and was getting well into our project. 'Special Brew' was in 'Olympic Studios' for about a week. In that short space of time, we saw Paul McCartney and Roger Taylor from 'Queen', who were both recording there. On one particular afternoon while in the middle of a session, someone came into our studio and asked us if they could show some visitors around. We agreed, and who should walk in but Robbie Krieger and 'The Doors'. The first thing he said to us was, 'Man, that's nice music'. He apologised for the interruption and said that he was looking for a suitable studio in England where he could record some of his new songs. He heard about 'Olympic Studios' in America, and was impressed with the reputation of its engineers. This boosted my ego, and looking back, it would have been the same for anyone else in my shoes.

We spent a couple of weeks listening to the tapes, and then Howard and I selected the final tracks. Howard had in fact financed the whole project, and had already gained an interest

OUTSIDE LOOKING IN

from a publisher friend in London. He thought it would be a good idea if I went to see him, so that we could discuss the band's future. I agreed, and a few weeks later a meeting was arranged. The band was getting excited, and they felt as if they were on the edge of a positive move towards fame and fortune. Personally, I was thrilled, but I have always been cautious and I never believe anything unless I can see it with my own eyes. Besides, any money owed to me has to be in my bank account and cleared before I do any further work for anyone. This is second nature for me, after having countless disappointments with endless bullshit from the music business.

I went to London to meet my publisher, Harold Shampan, who was part of the Dick James Organisation. At that time, Elton John had been signed to them. Harold seemed a decent guy, and had been in the business for many years. I trusted his judgement and felt very much at ease with him. He said that most of my songs were good, and that I was a talented writer. He thought that one or two of the songs certainly had the potential to be hit material. I was delighted to hear this, it was what every songwriter dreams of.

I came back from London that day on the train, and I couldn't remember the journey home. I wasn't drunk, I was just totally overwhelmed with the situation. As the next few weeks passed by, unknown to me, a big change was taking place behind the scenes. The once fashionable singer/songwriters, such as Elton John, Cat Stevens, and Gerry Rafferty, who had deep lyrics and strong melodies, were no longer in demand. To be honest, there was a glut of them, and the record business needed a fresh and different product. Obviously, the mood and attitude of the younger generation demanded this change. Our management company,

Pete Mitchell *alias* Stratmaster

'Elephant', laid on a party and we were all invited to the bash, with various celebrities milling around. We had Champagne and vol-au-vents in abundance, right slap bang in the middle of Piccadilly. We were being told how 'Special Brew' was going to be big and famous, and everyone was toasting us. Two weeks later, I went to London to collect some money owed to the band and got the surprise of my life. I walked into the reception area of 'Elephant Management' in Piccadilly, and the security guard asked me what I wanted. When I told him that I was looking for 'Elephant Management', he laughed and said, 'Oh they're not here mate, they've gone'. I asked him 'where?' and he said, 'under'. The annoying thing was that I never did get that money. This little escapade certainly made me more cautious with future management companies. My publisher, needless to say, was rather embarrassed with this management collapse. I discussed the matter with the band, and they were suggesting that perhaps the publisher might not be behind the project. In fact, they couldn't have been closer to the truth.

At a meeting with Harold soon after, we laid our cards on the table. I was nervous, and all I could think about was the future of the band. I was told that the Dick James Organisation liked my songs, believed in me, and was very happy to offer me a solo deal. They went on to say, 'we are aware that you have spent a lot of time working on this project with your band. Obviously, you are close to them, but in this business, you have to be realistic and have no hesitation in making a serious decision. We are talking about vast sums of money, and we are prepared to sign you up as a solo artiste, but we are no longer interested in your band. We are aware that you will need musicians, and we can get the best for you'. Immediately I froze, and there was a deadly silence. In other circumstances, this offer would have been ideal and I would

OUTSIDE LOOKING IN

have had no hesitation in saying 'Yes, please'. However, after spending so much time with these guys, working on the music, perfecting the songs, and then gigging live with the hope and belief that we were in it together, I just couldn't accept it. It was not a simple case of five guys playing together, we were like brothers.

I turned to Harold with tears in my eyes and said, 'Sorry, but I can't do it'. I have often wondered what would have happened if I had accepted their offer. I firmly believed that it was the right decision to make at that time. It was loyalty before success then. Looking back on it now, I think it was more like stupidity before necessity. I knew that one day I would pay the price for taking that stand. I have remained friends with Harold over the years, and he has given me advice and encouragement. I don't think he was surprised by my decision to refuse the offer. Eventually, Dick James, who had most of my songs signed to him, decided to put them all on the shelf. It would appear that because I wouldn't play ball with them, they were not going to do anything for me. In fact, the songs were kept for over nine years before I eventually got them released. The band's enthusiasm and spirit died instantly after that meeting, we all knew that it would never be the same again.

As I mentioned earlier, between 1976-77, a major change was taking place in the music world. On the music scene, we were experiencing a huge rebellion in attitude and fashion. This became the 'Punk Era', and record companies with their A&R people were changing their approach and rearranging their departments. Scouts were out looking for bands like the 'Sex Pistols' and the 'Damned'. This was obviously a serious blow to all the struggling singer/songwriters from the Cat

Pete Mitchell *alias* Stratmaster

Stevens and Elton John brigade. Sure enough, the change came, and there was an explosion of new bands with new ideas.

For the past few years, I had kept in touch with my producer, John Aster. He had been putting out various singles, some on his own labels. He always had his fingers in one thing or another. At the time, I think he was working on a record called 'Mouldy Old Dough', by Lieutenant Pigeon. I admired John. He never made the big time. He was a believer, and would work hard on a project if he liked what he heard on demo-tape. John was very experienced in the studio, and had spent years working on two- and four-track machines, and now was advanced with the new eight- and sixteen-track desks that were coming in. I arranged to see him one weekend and told him that I had a batch of songs, most in rough form on cassette. I played them to him, and got a positive reaction. I told John that I wanted to record an album, and that we could pick a dozen songs from that batch. He told me that he was broke, but would be prepared to hawk the demo-tapes around the business and see what sort of interest he could get and see what sort of deal he could find. Everywhere he went he got a mixed reaction, so we agreed that, ideally, we would at least deal for studio time. I would provide the songs and pay for the musicians, and the studio would have control of the finished master tape.

After a month or two punting around town, John eventually got a deal. It never ceases to amaze me just how small the music business is. He made a deal with Bernard Procter, who was the studio boss at "TMC Studios' in Mitcham. I remembered Bernie from way back in the early days. He owned the music shop where I bought my first electric guitar. It was

OUTSIDE LOOKING IN

called a Hofner 'Verithin', and was a semi-acoustic guitar. Bernie was also responsible for teaching me harmony vocals when I was a teenager back in the 'Centaur' days. Here he was, some fifteen years later, offering us a deal with his sixteen-track studio in Tooting. We went to the Indian restaurant opposite the studio and decided to have a meal. While eating our chicken curries and poppadoms, we discussed the deal and the contract. Bernie was making the most of it, and we eventually got down to brass tacks. We must have spent at least three hours eating and chatting in the restaurant, and I remember dreading the bill.

Finally, we made plans for the sessions, and Bemie gave us free studio time with an engineer. I agreed to provide the band and pay for any extra musicians should we need them. We worked hard for twelve weeks, doing all day and all night sessions, and rough mixes. Some of the tracks had top session players on them, like Gary Barnacle, Johnny Van Derrick, and Carl Wayne (The Move). This was my first serious attempt at a solo project, and I used the members of 'Special Brew' as the main band. Musically speaking, it was a fantastic experience for me, and it got the adrenaline flowing again.

Although my passion has always been to play live, I still enjoy working in the studio. It's a very creative environment for any musician to be in, especially if you are a songwriter. The tracks were going down, and we had ten songs near completion. Most of the tracks were different, due to the fact that we approached them individually. I had used different instruments on them, making sure that they didn't sound too similar. This can happen so easily to songs when penned by the same writer. I had harpsichord and mandolin on some songs, and saxophone with guitars on others. After about two weeks of mixing and re-mixing, we came out of the studio with the finished master tape. Now that we had the tape, all we had to do was get a deal for release and distribution with a record company.

John Aster went to every record company in London. Every time he came back he said, 'They thought it was great, but they only want one or two of the tracks'.

Nobody at that time was interested in doing a deal for the whole album. Bernie had made it quite clear that the deal had to be for the album in entirety. As time went on, this proved to be unobtainable, and it was to be another one of those so near and yet so far experiences, and certainly a big disappointment to all concerned. This was one more sixteen-track master tape left sitting on a shelf somewhere, collecting dust. The music scene was changing again, and we were witnessing the start of the 'Electronic Age'. I was beginning to realise that, once again, we had all missed the boat.

Ironically, Carl Wayne did say to me then that he would like to do a cover version of one of my songs called 'Read Between The Lines'. I must confess that at the time I wasn't too keen on the idea. Looking back, perhaps I should have agreed after all. It still would have been far better for at least one song to have seen the light of day than none of them. This is a common dilemma facing a performing writer, because he wants to have a successful hit song and record it himself, before anyone else. If you achieve that, then you are happy to let an established artiste record it later. In reality, the chance of it being a hit by an established artiste is far greater, because they have the record company backup, and a huge publicity machine already working for them. We certainly live and learn, and I have only one thing left to say, 'Come back Carl, all is forgiven'.

CHAPTER 6
THE ACID TEST

Having scratched around for eighteen months, gigging the pubs and any other paying gigs, I managed to save enough money to buy a house in Weybridge. I was heavily involved in writing songs, and I had finally come to terms with the record company rejections. Due to domestic pressures, my marriage to Jenny broke up, and on 22nd June, 1983 I was divorced. My kids were eleven and twelve years old and it was definitely the hardest and cruellest experience I had to endure. After a while, you know when things are not working in your relationship, and yet you still want to appear as if everything is fine in front of the kids. Your wife is doing more or less all the things a mother does, and still the kids detect a problem. They are so aware of the change in atmosphere and the change in one's tone of voice. All of this builds up inside of you, and it's so hard to carry on as if nothing has happened.

My break up was a gradual deterioration, caused by a number of things. For any musician who is trying to be successful, the last thing he needs is pressure from his marriage. It's the same for any businessman, he needs full support and encouragement from his partner. In fact, they say that behind every successful man is a good woman. I think the truth is more likely to be, how long is one prepared to wait for success? This is usually at the heart of the problem, and I have always had the attitude that I will carry on and be determined, no matter what. This is quite a tall order to expect from someone else, bearing in mind that it isn't their career. It doesn't end there, because apart from the marital problems, you have got the inevitable development of the kids. They demand your time and attention, just as much as the mother. In such a time-consuming business that is so unpredictable, I think it is impossible to be absorbed in it and go for it, if you have to carry the full responsibility of the family.

My honest opinion now is that anyone wanting to make it, whether it's in the music business or any other career, has first and foremost to be dedicated, with total belief in himself, and utterly selfish. He also has to be very lucky and determined, with a clear view of the direction he wants to go in, and not letting anyone or anything stand in his way. He has to be totally one-track minded, and, above all, he has got to have considerable talent.

Nothing compares with the pain and upset one goes through when your family falls apart.

I left Weybridge and moved in with my French girlfriend. She lived in Cobham with her son, Xavier, and she was waiting for her divorce. I was going through my separation at this time, and I needed some space to sort things out and get my head straight. I had various problems to sort out and being emotionally unbalanced wouldn't have helped matters. The kids were asking me tricky questions while I was going through the mill with all the court rigmarole. I remember my daughter, Mishka, sitting on my lap one evening just before I was about to leave home for the last time. She cuddled me and said, 'Daddy, why are you leaving us?' This has haunted me

OUTSIDE LOOKING IN

ever since. If you haven't experienced anything like this before, then you couldn't possibly know what real emotion is. My only thought at that time was to disappear and get as far away as possible from everybody and everything. In time, I knew that I was trying to run away from myself, because I hated what I was doing to my family. It didn't stop me from leaving, but I never intended to hurt anybody, certainly not my wife and kids. In order to sort my head out, I decided to get away and spend ten days with my girlfriend on the Channel Isles of Guernsey and Sark.

Sark is a small, beautiful island near Guernsey, and is totally unique. It is part of the Channel Islands with some very interesting features and a varied landscape. On one side of the island, there are farms. Across the other side, there are rocks and coves with sandy beaches. It has its own community and character, and has to be one of the most natural places I have ever seen. There are no cars allowed on the island, so you have to travel around by horse and cart or bicycle, unless you prefer to walk. A few ride around on tractors, but they are the local folk who work on the farms.

I spent four days on Sark, and I was so impressed with the feel of the place that I had to write a song about it. Both of us were able to unwind, and we spent the rest of the time on Guernsey talking and working things out. Both of us knew that we had one hell of a lot to sort out when we got back home. First thing on the agenda were the kids. I had Mishka and Tyler to see, and Françoise had her son, Xavier, to sort out. All three kids were badly shaken up, and they became our main priority. Xavier became friends with Mishka and Tyler, and eventually they all went to the same school. When Xavier was younger, I taught him to play the guitar. I also showed

Pete Mitchell *alias* Stratmaster

Tyler a few things on the guitar. They have both grown up with it, and, in my opinion, they can both play very well. I moved into Cobham with Françoise.

Now it was time to get my career sorted out. I wanted to play my own songs a lot more, especially around the circuit. Over the past few years, I had collected quite a few original songs for my catalogue, some from the 'Special Brew' days, and some more recent. I have never stopped writing, as it tends to come in phases, and I always have something to say. Right now, I was thinking very seriously about a brand-new venture, something that I hadn't tried before. So far, I had always been in a band with four or five members, playing gigs around the circuit. For some time I had wanted to go out and perform as a solo singer/songwriter. Personally, I knew that this would be the biggest challenge I could have. It would be a very different approach, and I would have to plan it carefully, and with a good deal of thought.

In the summer of 1982, I embarked on a solo project, and it was probably the most nerve-wracking thing I have ever done. I was concentrating much more now on writing and performing my own songs. Everything pointed in this direction, and there would be far less chance, I thought, of anything going wrong. With just myself to consider, there would be no more problems with drunken players or hanging around waiting for late arrivals. Quite simply put, there would be no more headaches. I would have everything more or less under my control. Just imagine, no more bickering for a while, and no more listening to everyone else's likes and dislikes, when all you want to do is have some fun and get up and play. I was very keen on the idea of going solo, and I have to admit that all the advantages at this point seemed to be very attractive.

OUTSIDE LOOKING IN

My first move was to plan and arrange the new solo act. I called myself 'The Minstrel', and played throughout the south of England for about two years. I must have gigged well over two hundred wine bars and pubs during that period of time. From the playing aspect, as any reasonable guitarist would know, there had to be a very different approach with the guitar, especially with the playing techniques. Having spent my earlier years serving my apprenticeship playing acoustic guitars, I was able to draw from that experience, and I felt that the only way I would get the sound that I wanted would be to use a twelve-string electric/acoustic guitar.

I bought myself an Ovation 'Pacemaker', and I used it through a Roland echo unit. This was the RE 501, and it gave me mainly echo and chorus effects. The vocals and guitar went into an eight hundred watt Peavey sound system in stereo. By using a twelve-channel desk, I could pre-set the channels. Françoise, who was my sound engineer at the time, would select the right channel to suit the song played. Suddenly I realised that going solo did have its disadvantages after all. One of the more obvious ones being it is very easy to sound the same all night on every song, and even easier to sound empty and thin. This is mainly due to the contrast of playing with a band one minute, and then playing on your own the next. It takes a while for the ears to appreciate the space around the songs. In many cases I think this has been the make or break for solo acts. How many times have you walked into a venue and heard someone strumming a guitar and singing on their own, and then after five minutes, you've had enough and can't wait to get out? This is the problem, it sounds all right for five minutes, but two hours—forget it!

At last I was playing five nights a week across the south of England. The venues were very different from the pub circuits that I had been used to. I was playing a lot more wine-bars and bistros. Playing as a solo act was a very different ball game. In order to avoid becoming another five-minute bore, I had to make my songs interesting and varied. I worked hard on the light and shade aspect, using the space to enhance the songs, and my guitar techniques were varied. On some of the songs, I used a pick with full rock sounds, and on others, I played finger-style with soft melodic tones. Most of the songs were originals, with a few covers mixed in. In order to avoid boredom, I had to vary my vocal approach. On one song I would sing a hard rock vocal similar to Bob Segar, and then I would follow it with a softer song by Cat Stevens.

After some fine-tuning and invaluable help from Françoise on the desk, I started to build up a solid and varied two-hour repertoire as a solo act. When it was working right, the satisfaction and personal buzz was unequalled. I think that this is without doubt the ultimate test for any singer/songwriter, to go out on your own with just voice and guitar. This was the real nitty gritty, and I knew that if I could crack this, I would be able to cope with anything. There is no hiding place and nobody to hold your hand, you are out there on your own. I have to say at this stage that without the total support and constant encouragement from Françoise, my solo career would never have worked.

Some of my experiences were just amazing, and I believe it worked for me for a number of reasons. Remember, 'YOU ARE ONLY AS GOOD AS YOU SOUND'. I had first class equipment and all the commitment in the world, plus the full backup at every gig from Françoise. She was working on the mixing desk balancing the sounds in a noisy and smoky environment. Putting up with drunks who were slobbering all over the place was not an easy task for anybody. Once I was singing a love song in front of some drunks, and they were shouting abuse at us, deliberately trying to distract me and

OUTSIDE LOOKING IN

break my concentration. They were stoned out of their skulls and looking for attention, probably thinking, who better to annoy than me? The show always went on, and usually by the time the gig finished, the drunks had gone home. In another club, I was singing a very emotional song while staring into the faces of people who were stuffing spaghetti and food into their mouths. This is the reality of working as a solo performer in hotels and particularly in restaurants.

On a more encouraging note, there were some great moments. I played at the 'Lazy Toad' club in Gravesend on one occasion to a full house. After every song, I was bombarded with money, people were just throwing it at me. What really excited me was the fact that I was playing original songs. Later, while working at a bar in Harrow, I had another remarkable experience. I was sitting inside the front bay window on stage, where you could see me playing from the road outside the bar. On this particular night, we had a fair crowd, and I was playing through my first set. Halfway through, I saw a beautiful white Rolls-Royce saloon pull up outside. I noticed a young couple come into the bar, impeccably dressed. They sat down for a while and listened to my songs. I finished the set and took a break. As I got up to get a beer, the guy who had arrived in the white Rolls came over to me. He said I had made his evening, and that he had thoroughly enjoyed listening to the music. He then pushed a roll of notes into my hand, and I was completely stunned. I said I was delighted that he had enjoyed the songs, and that, really, he had made my night.

Working with Françoise was a very special time, and we had some laughs. It meant that while I was on stage playing, I was on my own. For the rest of the time, we were together, and that was really enjoyable. We were a complete team, and we would plan every gig beforehand. We traveled around in a Citroen 'Dyane', and in order to get all the gear in, we had to

Pete Mitchell *alias* Stratmaster

pack it just right. Everything had its place, and we had a lot of gear to carry. I did most of the driving and Françoise took care of the maps and routes. Whenever we were out in the middle of winter, we would take a survival kit with us, consisting of cheese sandwiches and hot coffee. We were never too keen to eat in the motorway cafes, for obvious culinary reasons. The amazing thing was that we drove thousands of miles in that little Citroen car, and we only broke down once.

Françoise and I had just finished a gig in Romsey, near Southampton, when we came out of the pub at midnight. I fumed the ignition and the car wouldn't start, which was very unusual, it normally started straight away. Eventually, after a few attempts, I managed to get it going and off we went. Ten minutes later, I noticed that the lights were getting dimmer, and it was affecting the running of the engine. I immediately thought that the battery was faulty, and so I pulled up and kept the engine running. I didn't want to drain the battery any more by starting it up again. Nevertheless, it was slowly deteriorating and the battery was losing its charge. All I could do was switch the headlights on to sidelights, and turn off the heater. Rapidly, I became unpopular, and we couldn't see where we were going. We started to get cold and irritable, but we kept our spirits up and managed to get a police escort to the next garage. We were now able to buy a new battery and solve the problem, and, what is more, we got home safely.

After working for nearly two years as the 'Minstrel', I had played in all kinds of bars. In 'Rosies' of Worthing, while playing to a frenzied crowd, punters joined in with me on stage. I played to all kinds of people, from 'Skinheads' and 'Royalty' in Exeter, to seamen and dockers in Gravesend. There were students in Oxford and Bath, with stag and hen nights, cross-channel ferries, and even charity gigs. In all honesty, I played to anyone prepared to listen, because I knew the experience

OUTSIDE LOOKING IN

was going to be invaluable to my personal development. What I gained from this adventure was a far greater awareness of the audience.

When you are solo, you cannot drift off into a self-indulgency thing. You either get it right the first time, or you DIE ON YOUR FACE.

CHAPTER 7
FINAL DRIVE

Seeing my thirty-ninth birthday on the horizon made me feel restless. I was getting that familiar feeling once again, the one where you think that the grass could be greener on the other side of the fence. This seemed to be part of an ongoing philosophy for me, a sort of carrot for the donkey. With the constant need to gig, I felt that the time was right to put together a new band, one with a difference. Perhaps one that would play, more or less, the songs I had been doing as a solo artiste. I also wanted to include songs from the 'Special Brew' days, and ones that I had written throughout the 'Minstrel' period. After a few more rejection letters from record companies with their 'It's not quite what we are looking for' remarks, and the continual frustration of having my songs tied up with dormant publishers, I thought it was high time to air these songs to an audience. After all said and done, that is the whole point of writing them in the first place. Fired up and ready, I advertised for musicians to join my new band. We called it 'Hustler', and within six weeks, we were in rehearsals. After a few more weeks, we had a couple of sets arranged and we were ready to gig. Self managed and financed, we started to gig around the pub and club circuits.

OUTSIDE LOOKING IN

There is always a catch to any significant move in this business, particularly when large sums of money are at stake. Nobody does anything for nothing, but everybody wants something for nothing. Sure enough, this was to surface within the 'Hustler' camp. The snag was to get the musicians to take a chance and gamble on the band. A certain card had to be placed on the table, this card being in the form of a record deal. Yes, that famous old chestnut we have all heard, time and time again, in the music business... **THE DEAL.**

This places an immediate pressure on the writer of the band, who has to convince all and sundry that he has the winning songs. Having got over that hurdle, he then has to gun for it, looking for any interested party in the record business. I am sure you must realise by now that to survive as a low-key working musician, one has to be able to adapt and master the proverbial art of ducking and diving. 'Hustler' played on the circuit for a few months, building up interest in the songs and getting some good crowds. Every time we played at the 'Bacchus' club in Bournemouth, they had to close the doors early, and the place would be rocking until 1am in the morning.

When we weren't gigging, I would be out searching for a deal of some kind, or record company interest. I sent a tape to WEA (UK), and to my surprise, I received a reply almost immediately. They said they were interested in the songs, and in one song in particular. This song was called 'Survive', and I had been playing it at the gigs with 'Hustler'. We were getting some good press write-ups, and the A&R team from WEA (UK) wanted to see the band in action. We arranged a showcase gig at the 'Bun Shop' in Surbiton, The local press came along with the A&R people from WEA (UK). It was a great atmosphere, and we had some excellent lighting and effects laid on. I thought that the band played great and, more impor-

Pete Mitchell *alias* Stratmaster

tantly, that the songs came across well. It appeared that a good time was had by all. Soon after, I was called to a meeting in London to discuss the possibility of recording the song, 'Survive'. Apparently, WEA (UK) was keen, but, after negotiations with WEA (USA), who was in control of the purse strings, they decided to pass on it. This was another case of one more crack at it, followed by one more big disappointment.

You can imagine that by now, I had become a total cynic, but nevertheless, it was something that I was getting more and more used to as time went on. In this business, there are never any set rules. I immediately switched into a different mode, and put all my energy and thoughts into my gigs, focussing on the LIVE aspect of the business. I must admit, deep down I was really sick and tired of looking for deals in the UK. I have always been a realist, and touching forty years of age meant that I would have to be even more realistic.

The amount of artistes over forty that get signed up in the UK could be counted on one hand. 'Hustler' was a very short experience, but it did manage to get a track released, and that was on the 'Thameside Story' album. The song was called 'Born A Leo', and I wrote it especially for that album. Everything I try to do musically has to have a purpose. No matter how small the result, I have always managed to achieve some kind of personal satisfaction. This is obviously driven by the urge to play, and the point is, that one doesn't have to be famous to feel this way. Often lethargy can creep in through the back door of fame and fortune.

After whetting my appetite, I wanted to take things a step further. I had been playing original songs with a band that was only motivated by a record deal. Because of this, I wanted to get a band together with guys like myself. I wanted people who

OUTSIDE LOOKING IN

were on my wavelength, musicians who were not working full-time in day jobs. I wanted guys that were available anytime to go anywhere and play, even if the money was tight. It's a known fact that you either play the big time for record companies, or you play pubs and clubs for peanuts, as I have been doing for years. There is no in-between, it simply doesn't exist.

The pub circuit is a real pig of an animal, or, as I would say, snake in the grass. Just when you think that you've got it sussed, you realise that you haven't. Nobody takes the responsibility for anything, and there are more cock-ups and double bookings going on than anywhere else in 'Showbiz Land'. The house public address system in most pubs is usually worse than the local fairground. The majority of pubs were designed for tables and chairs, not for live bands. Often bands are squashed and cooped up in impossible areas to produce amazing sounds of Albert Hall quality, when in reality they have to play in a rabbit hutch with Turkish bath acoustics. Sometimes they have to play without a stage area, coupled with poor lighting and bad earthing. In some places, they want you to keep the toilet doors clear, or allow access to the cigarette machines and amusements. Once we had a situation where the pool table remained in use throughout the gig, and another where the television was left on with some kind of sport blaring out. We have even had the jukebox playing at exactly the same time as the band. How about that? Just to really put the boot in, one could go through all of this crap, and then end up in a pub where the decor was so depressive that it felt like a derelict barn.

It has taken me over twenty years of surveying to find enough suitable pubs, but when you do, it makes it all worthwhile. The thing I have noticed about the good pubs is that they nearly always have a decent landlord or landlady. What is more, they always give you a free beer. Isn't life strange? You will rarely see any contract for a pub venue, but you will often be asked to sign a brewery form as a receipt before you get your money. The pubs are the same as record companies, they want it all in their favour.

It has, and always will be, the poor old musician at the end of the day who stands to lose more than anybody. Because of this, I have always tried to steer clear of agents, and very few of them, in my opinion, are worth the effort. The point being, pub gigs pay very small fees, and there is very little profit for any agent who is just taking his ten percent. An interesting thing about live music on the pub scene is that if any other business operated like it and treated its employees as badly as they do the bands, nobody would work for them. There would be an all out strike and I think many other businesses would simply go under.

Of course, I realise that the pubs have got to sell their beer, but a lot of these pubs, quite frankly, would be empty every night without live music, and what is more, they know it! I think live music and beer go together like bread and cheese. The funny thing is, I've been around as long as many of these landlords, and probably longer than most, and I've seen this whole scenario go round full circle more than once. Some of the pubs have had three or four landlords come and go since I started playing. I have experienced working for all kinds of landlords and agents, and it's true to say that I have met some decent ones, but more often than not, they are usually pretty indifferent, and a few of them are quite pathetic. You know the ones, they think that they're doing you a big favour, and you get the other kind who think that they're showbiz entrepreneurs, and 'Big Time' promoters, when the sad truth is, that most of them couldn't even organise a simple Friday night quiz.

OUTSIDE LOOKING IN

Quite a significant change took place on the music scene in the summer of 1988. I had a feeling that this would happen, because the electronic boom had dominated the eighties, and nine out of ten acts were using electronic gadgetry. This was really a substitute for musicians, and from my point of view, the worst thing that could have happened to the live music scene. The working musician suffered, and pubs were booking 'one man bands' geared up with effects, trying to sound like full bands. Of course, the pubs only had to pay out wages for one man. This was brought home to me time and time again throughout my solo career. The bottom line was that even a small band would cost three times as much. Work was harder to find through the eighties, but nevertheless I still carried on working. I just had to be more adaptable, and play gigs and clubs that I wouldn't normally have played by choice. Working mens' clubs particularly spring to mind, always good facilities, but dreadful audiences with screaming kids running all over the place.

The thing about the clubs is that they are usually self-financed, and operate on a membership basis. Members can take guests and sign them in, which obviously entails a membership fee. The club usually has a committee, which runs the administration and management side of things, and it nearly always has an entertainments manager. His role is to sort out the booking of the bands and various acts throughout the year, besides taking care of the finance and payments. To be honest, I have always judged a club by the entertainments manager. If he's got his act together and knows exactly what he wants and when, then there is a good chance it will be a good club with a good crowd. This usually meant that there was a very good chance of a successful gig. If you had an idiot running the club, then God help you.

Pete Mitchell *alias* Stratmaster

Often we would arrive at a working mens' club, only to find that while we had been booked in to play our type of music, they were expecting something else. It's not much fun having to play to a crowd of people who are not the slightest bit interested in what you are playing. People request songs by artistes you've never heard of, and songs that you wouldn't be seen dead playing. No matter what you do to compromise, you're on a hiding to nothing. Like most venues, the clubs have their favourite acts, and they can be very cold towards a new act, especially when it comes into their territory for the first time. They take great delight in being critical, and are very quick to put you down. It's not easy to play Rock and Roll to people with pacemakers, and even harder if they are wearing hearing aids.

Having said that, when you eventually do get booked into the right venue and accepted, it can be a very good night. I think that the clubs are being taken over gradually by the younger generation, and they are becoming much more relaxed and Rock and Roll influenced. Hopefully this trend will continue, and we will have a lot more venues available for Blues musicians. As I said earlier, there is always a catch to everything in this business, and I don't think that will ever change.

Realising that a change was taking place and that a lot more youngsters were appreciating live music, I decided to put together a brand new pub band. Having been weaned on the Blues and Rock and Roll, my number one passion has always been playing electric Blues guitar. A good friend of mine, Chris New, joined me on second guitar. After various auditions, we found a bass and drummer. Ironically, none of the musicians auditioned were suitable, the bassist and drummer that did eventually settle in were old friends of mine and had worked with me previously. John Bulpitt, the bassist, came

OUTSIDE LOOKING IN

from 'Hustler', and Stuart James, our drummer, had worked with me in the studio back in the 'Special Brew' days. Once again, this proves that a good band depends on its chemistry and the players need to know each other inside out. This is probably the main ingredient for a successful recipe. We called the band 'Four Wheel Drive' and it had a specific plan and direction. We wanted to work around the pub circuits and play our own brand of Rhythm and Blues. We didn't want to be too purist, but, at the same time we still wanted to play songs by some of the old Blues artistes like Freddie King, John Lee Hooker and Muddy Waters. In 1972, I met Muddy Waters at IBC studios in London. He was recording his 'London Sessions'. From that moment on, I knew that there was definitely a place for the harder-edged Blues. As a tribute to Muddy, we played the old Willie Dixon track called 'I'm Ready'. We are really talking about mixing the Chicago Blues with the Texas Blues. Modern players, such as the late Stevie Ray Vaughan, would be a good example for variation in song tempo, are an important factor to the Blues-based repertoire.

Pubs nearly always want cover songs, and very few want Indies bands. Most of the punters want to relate to the songs and have a good time. They're not necessarily musicians, and they're certainly not A&R people from record companies looking for original bands to sign up. 'Four Wheel Drive' worked solidly from 1988-1999 on the pub and club circuits. The gigs always varied, and some were far more enjoyable than others.

We had a couple of gigs from one agent at this time, and at one of them, we had to stand in at short notice for 'Cliff Bennett and the Rebel Rousers'. It was on New Year's Eve. Apparently they pulled out at the last minute, and we were asked to do it. The money was good, but everybody there kept asking us to play the Rebel Rousers' hits, and sure enough we

Pete Mitchell *alias* Stratmaster

DIDN'T. To their surprise, we played our own music instead and bluffed our way through to the halfway break. At this point, the manager of the club called me into his office, and I had to tell him that we were 'Four Wheel Drive', and that we had been booked at the last minute to save the day.

Fortunately, he accepted my explanation, and we got paid. I also got a nice thank you note from the agent for getting him out of the soup. On another occasion, we were asked to back 'Wee Willie Harris' at a club in Kent. On this particular evening, we were waiting at the bar, ready to go on in about thirty minutes, and there was no sign of 'Wee Willie Harris'. With about twenty minutes to go, he came into the pub and went upstairs. I followed him up, and while he was changing, he gave me a rundown of his repertoire, and I had exactly ten minutes to rehearse it in. What made it even trickier was the fact that he gave me a huge pile of sheet music and said, 'There it is, and can I have a fanfare for my intro?' Apparently, he always came on stage with a fanfare. I flicked through the sheet music quickly and worked out a fanfare for him on the spot. At the end of the evening, 'Wee Willie Harris' thanked us for a great night and gave us all a signed photograph, what a nice bloke.

'Four Wheel Drive' played private gigs, Dover ferries, and, in June 1992, we played at the famous Burstin Hotel in Folkstone to an age group I would prefer to forget. Having said that, they rocked and rolled as good as anyone, with great appreciation. Nothing stays the same for long, life has this habit of changing, and for the last couple of years, Chris, our second guitarist, had been having problems. Yes, you've guessed it... domestic ones! I have to say I have seen many a good musician bite the dust, usually because of a troubled relationship. Having said this, we all have to get on with our own situations in life, for some it is going to be tougher than for others. Personally, I've had to go through years of making sacrifices, and it would seem that this is really the price you have to pay to PLAY.

I have become quite cynical regarding this situation, and I don't have much time for sympathy. You have to find a way of compromising, because if your loyalties lie elsewhere and you let the side down, what happens to the band? Strange but true, as soon as Chris left the band, his relationship broke up and he was living on his own. As we gigged through 1994, things were reaching a head and Chris was finding it tough going. He was taking his problems with him to the gigs, and this inevitably led to the rest of us feeling uncomfortable, with a few heated moments. You can't spend all that time traveling around in a van for hours on end listening to someone who is screwed up, without reacting to it. Once or twice, it came near to blows, and that, for me, was the red light. After a good chat, Chris decided that it would be best for all concerned if he were to pull out.

We were left with two choices, bearing in mind that we had a diary full of gigs for 1995. We could either find a replacement and stay a four piece all-guitar band, or we could completely re-design the band and turn it into a three-piece unit. We decided to do the latter for the following reasons. First, financially we would benefit immediately, a sort of pay rise. Secondly, we would have a lot more room to set up and play in on stage. Thirdly, the van had been designed with three seats, and finally, most of the venues preferred a three-piece band. Pubs feel less intimidated and are happy to pay less. I suppose when you actually stop and think about it, a pub's priority is to sell beer, and any landlord will soon tell you this. I always take this into the equation whenever I am arranging new gigs. We all know that if they don't sell their beer, you don't go back. Having decided unanimously, by democratic

Pete Mitchell *alias* Stratmaster

vote, to become a three-piece band, we arranged to have another one of our many pub meetings. We knew that we would have to re-design the repertoire, and so we spent a couple of afternoons in rehearsals and sorted out most of the songs. Some of them had to be dropped, and a few were rearranged. To make up the sets, we brought in some new songs and eventually we were ready to gig. I was amazed at how quickly this band came together, in fact, we didn't have to cancel any gigs throughout the change-over period.

Becoming a three-piece band was a real kick up the backside for all of us. From a musical point of view, not having that second guitar meant I would have to play lead guitar and cover rhythm guitar at the same time. The bass would have to be much more versatile and rhythmic, and the drummer would have to adjust his rhythm patterns and techniques. We suddenly noticed a lot more space in the sound, and this was in fact a real bonus. Apart from sorting out the men from the boys, it forced us to play better and with more attention to details. It put much more focus on the light and shade aspect of things. I believe that because of this, the band is now playing better than ever. At the meeting, we decided to change the band's name from 'Four Wheel Drive', to DRIVE.

Punters for a tape were constantly asking 'DRIVE', and obviously, any band looking for work needs a good tape. The band was ready to record an album, and when we recorded the tape, we made it absolutely clear that it would have to be a tape that sounded exactly the same as we did live. This would mean using only one guitar, with bass and drums, without any further overdubs. There are so many bands that get in the studio and put everything down on the tape. They use up all the tracks, leaving no space or separation in the sound. Worst of all, they end up with a tape sounding very different from their live sound, and then they wonder why they're not re-booked.

OUTSIDE LOOKING IN

On 17th October, 1999, we went into the studio to record the album, and a good friend of mine engineered the sessions. Within three days, it was recorded and mixed. We then had it mastered onto DAT. Our tapes were copied from DAT, and the album was called 'TANKED UP'. After all the hard work, everybody involved was pleased with the result. Recording within a set budget is always a difficult task, but at the end of the day, you have to end up with an acceptable tape. Eventually, the artwork for the cassette inlay was designed and printed and we ended up with a great tape in a well-presented package. We are currently selling our 'Tanked Up' album at all our gigs, and we are being asked now for the follow up.

Looking ahead, we have gigs booked in, and we are going to record a new CD for the punters in the New Year. In this business, you have to take what comes when it comes, and with both feet firmly on the ground, even though there is a definite element of excitement about the unknown. As a band, we still think about success in some form or another, and I am writing new songs all the time. As far as the band is concerned, it is an ongoing commitment, and who knows what lies around the corner? The truth is that if I was caught up in a 9-5 syndrome, I probably would have gone mad by now and committed to an asylum.

It would appear that the whole 'DRIVE' concept was a good move. Within the first year, we have been fortunate enough to play Blues festivals and pretty much all the main pub venues in the south. It has been one hell of a long road, sometimes downhill, but, more often than not, a hard uphill struggle. What keeps you going and drives you along are the rare exceptional gigs. Some gigs are remembered for their success and status, and other gigs become markers in time.

Pete Mitchell *alias* Stratmaster

From many of the experiences I've had over the years, the biggest shock so far was on Saturday, the 13th, May 1995, when DRIVE was playing at a bar called 'Scratchers' in Famcombe, Surrey. I was on stage, and we were just about to start our first song.

As I was about to strike the first note, a young guy stood right in front of me and I froze. I looked at him closely, and he said to me, 'You know who I am don't you?'

I said, 'You certainly look familiar, who are you?'

Bursting into a smile and grabbing hold of me he said, 'You should know me, I'm your brother'!

I have to tell you I was completely numb throughout the whole of the first set. My vision was blurred and I had to switch into automatic pilot. The reason being that I hadn't seen my one and only younger brother, John, for almost nine years. Sadly, we had never really gotten to know each other, and I'm sure that it's mainly due to the age difference.

This was just another one of those many sacrifices I had to make throughout my career. Now my brother and I are closer than ever. To my delight, he is trying hard to establish himself as a pub musician, playing with his own rock band on the circuit. Above all, he said he was very impressed with 'DRIVE', and that meant everything to me. For both me and the band, our attitude is always the same. Wherever we play, whether it's the 'Dog and Duck', or 'Wembly Stadium', we will give it absolutely everything. You never know, it could suddenly be the last gig for any of us, and the one thing that we have to get out of it is the inner satisfaction and unexplainable buzz that feeds our soul. I can only speak for myself, but the feeling one gets from playing live on stage, regardless of where you are, is

OUTSIDE LOOKING IN

probably best described as being ten times better than any orgasm. My view is that it is truly unequalled, and when you finish a gig, you are left with a huge vacuum inside your stomach. You feel like a screwed-up paper bag, totally drained, and after any gig it usually takes me a couple of hours to wind down. I can get home at 2 or 3am in the morning, and I'm always tired and hungry. The worst thing is that the brain is so active that it's impossible to go straight to sleep.

So when you think about it, a typical pub gig can entail loading the van at 5pm and then arriving home at 3am in the morning. You are talking about a ten-hour slog, but the actual playing time on stage, which is really the icing on the cake, is only about two hours. How many people realise what is involved when they go to see a pub band? Apart from the van maintenance, gear maintenance, stage clothes being washed and ironed, and stringing instruments, there is a heap of work to be done on the management side of things, and I have always handled this gruelling task myself. Very few pub bands have got serious management, the money simply isn't there to justify it.

A typical day for me can be spent writing and sending out posters to gigs. One can spend hours on the phone wheeling and dealing and going out on the road punting for work, touting pubs and talking directly to the landlords. Advertising the band is also time consuming, and then the local papers and music press have to be informed about our gigs. We also have to notify the radio stations and send out tapes and P/R (Public Relations) packages to new venues. On top of this, one still has to find the time to get down to some serious songwriting. If you held a day job, you would never have the time to run a full-time pub band. My attitude has always been that someone has to do it, and that someone is usually me. I think that with such an insecure business, I've got to feel in control. By doing it myself, I gain a feeling of security. I always remember my father saying to me as a kid, 'The only security you've got in this life, son, is yourself.

'DRIVE' is an ongoing force. It is a band that for me represents over thirty years of graft and sweat on the showbiz fringes, never quite making the 'Big Time'. Who knows? Perhaps I have already had the cream, and I'm only just realising it.

People often ask me, 'How long will you continue to travel down this soul-destroying road?'

My answer has always been the same, and that is, 'Until I lose that burning desire to play'.

What I would say to any budding pub musician, with tongue firmly planted in cheek, is: If you're prepared to be flexible and play in an area hardly big enough to peel an orange in for a mean, long-faced publican who would much rather you'd left your gear in the van, then you might just have a slim chance of being 'pub entertainer of the year'. As far as surviving in a Rock and Roll band on the pub circuit is concerned, don't kid yourself, you haven't even started.

What I do find rather amusing is that for years we have heard so much about the 'drugs, sex, and Rock and Roll', and what I'd really like to know is, 'What happened to the DRUGS AND SEX?'

Alas, I've got to sign off now and put some oil in the van, string my guitar, load up my gear, check the route for tonight's gig, and, if I've got any energy left, get to the gig and ROCK THEIR SOCKS OFF. Remember, Keep on rocking, it's the only way to survive, especially if you're—OUTSIDE LOOKING IN.

OUTSIDE LOOKING IN

SUPPLEMENTARY BENEFITS—
THAT WE COULD WELL
DO WITHOUT.

1. The famous drunk who says he can sing and play, and then, wait for it, better than you, and, what's more, he has backed everybody from 'Elvis' to 'East 1' and then his finale is usually a painful rendition of 'Danny Boy'.

2. Requests for Country and Western songs, or, anything else irrelevant to your style.

3. Ridiculous playing areas that aren't big enough for solo acts, let alone bands.

4. Mean and moody landlords who wouldn't dream of buying you a beer. But then, why should they? They're already paying you a mere pittance.

5. The so-called guitar expert who knows more about your guitar than you do, and any other guitar for that matter. Mind you, he can't play a note... sad really.

6. Pubs with gents' conveniences, where you stand up to your ankles in urine. There is no towel, no soap, no loo paper and not even any hot water.

7. The microphone meddler, who, for some strange reason, can't keep his hands off the microphone. It's like a magnet, he's just got to mess with it. If you're really lucky, you might get one who treats you to an 'Elvis' impersonation.

8. The frustrated guitarist who wants to play your guitar—at his peril.

Pete Mitchell *alias* Stratmaster

9. The frustrated drummer who has been wetting himself all night, longing for the chance to creep up behind the kit and beat hell out of the first drum he can lay his hands on, not realising that it's probably the closest he'll ever come to being murdered in his local by the drummer.

10. The drunken dancer, who seems to move with his brain totally detached from his body, causing more damage than a demolition crew. Funny thing is they never seem to know when to stop.

11. Pubs with poor lighting. Everybody thinks there has been a power cut. It's either pitch black inside, or the spotlights blind you.

12. The P/A scam (public address system), where the publican says that you have to use his superb sound system, but when you sound check—it's horrendous, and then he's got the nerve to charge you for the suffering you've had to endure.

13. The decibel meter. This crafty little device is strategically placed to keep the volume under control, but it has a nasty habit of cutting off the power supply when you're halfway through a song.

OUTSIDE LOOKING IN

LANDLORD'S LEXICON— WHY DON'T THEY SAY WHAT THEY MEAN?

1. Says... What kind of following have you got?
   Means... This isn't really a music pub.

2. Says... How much more gear have you got to bring in?
   Means... At this rate there will be no room left for the punters.

3. Says... We don't have live music here very often.
   Means... We don't have a music licence.

4. Says... It's very quiet here tonight.
   Means... We won't be booking you again.

5. Says... Any chance in playing one more?
   Means... I like a band that earns their money.

6. Says... We have had a few complaints from the neighbours recently.
   Means... I hope that you're not going to be too loud tonight.

7. Says... Things have been pretty slow just lately.
   Means... There will be no free drinks tonight'

8. Says... The punters are in early tonight.
   Means... I think it's time you started playing.

Pete Mitchell *alias* Stratmaster

9. Says... They like all kinds of music here.
   Means... I don't mind what you play, as long as we sell the beer.

10. Says... I'm looking forward to a nice early night tonight.
    Means... Don't even think about late night drinks.

Printed in the United Kingdom
by Lightning Source UK Ltd.
109620UKS00001BA/1